THE O

COMPUTER

HATER'S

HANDBOOK

THE OFFICIAL
COMPUTER
HATER'S
HANDBOOK

AT LAST! A COMPUTER BOOK FOR EVERYONE WHO DOESN'T KNOW
AND DOESN'T CARE HOW THE DAMN THINGS WORK.

D.J. Arneson

A DELL TRADE PAPERBACK

Other Dell titles by D. J. Arneson:
The Original PREPPY Jokebook
The Original PREPPY Cookbook

A DELL TRADE PAPERBACK

Published by
Dell Publishing Co., Inc.
1 Dag Hammarskjold Plaza
New York, New York 10017

Dell® TM 681510, Dell Publishing Co., Inc.

Printed in the United States of America

First printing — July 1983

ISBN: 0-400-56619-3

ACKNOWLEDGMENTS

Many brilliant minds must share the blame for *The Official Computer Hater's Handbook*. Some are more guilty than others. Of course, the initial debt of gratitude, as in *"Thanks a lot,"* must go to the meddlers of history who simply couldn't leave well enough alone and insisted on counting things (see page 16, for example).

Considering the havoc numbers, counting, calculation and, now, computing have wrought on Mankind, it was probably the Devil himself who first came up with the concept of numbering things. "Have an apple," he said to Eve. "In fact, take two, one for each of you."

Once the notion that things could be counted and calculated appeared, others with equally Mephistophelean mindsets added their own devilment to further confuse a world up to then getting along just fine with "more," "less," and "I dunno."

And so, to men like Euclid for his geometry, Zeno for his paradoxes, Archimedes for calculating *pi*, Descartes for analytical geometry, Newton and Leibniz for their infinitesimal calculus, Lobachevski and Bolyai for their non-Euclidean geometry, Riemann for his geometry, Pascal for his little calculating machine, Babbage for his big calculating machine, Hollerith for his punched cards, Zuse for his primitive computer, Boole for his 1's and 0's, Shockley et al for their transistors, and Kilby and Noyce for their microchips, credit must here be given, for without them there would be no computers, and, therefore, no *Official Computer Hater's Handbook*.

Others who are not totally blameless for *The Official Computer Hater's Handbook* are Beatrice Arneson, my personal source, who keeps feeding me ideas for books, my incredible sons, Leif and Marc, who keep me humble, Phillip Brown, who designed the book and Mary Ellen Brown, who provided constant help; also, Milt Oehler for his foresight, Bob Mecoy for his uncommon editorial patience, Martha Brown, Comptype, Jose Delbo, Avery Brannaka, Barry Kroke, and Epson America, Inc. for the Amazing Epson QX-10, a computer that's so friendly, it's a computer even an Official Computer Hater can love. And finally, the entire class of 1953 at Montevideo (Minn.) High School who needed somebody to be better than at math, and chose me. Florence Kjelsberg, where are you now when I *need* you?

CONTENTS

CHAPTER ONE

The History of Computers

CHAPTER TWO

Computer Personae

CHAPTER THREE

The Computer Business

CHAPTER FOUR

Valley Boys

CHAPTER FIVE

Word Processing

CHAPTER SIX

Computer Spread

CHAPTER SEVEN

Hardware, Software and Nowhere

CHAPTER EIGHT

ComputerSpeak

FOR MICKEY

THE HISTORY OF COMPUTERS

IF WE ONLY KNEW THEN WHAT WE KNOW NOW

Chapter One

IN THE BEGINNING

The Origin of the Infernal Machine

Computers are to the Technological Revolution what the steam engine was to the Industrial Revolution — and you know what happened when steam replaced the horse. Millions of horses out of work.

The same thing is happening today, before our very eyes. If the Technological Revolution continues apace, everybody is going to be out of work before the year 2000, except the programmers. The rest of us will be en- ▷

slaved by their infernal machines, glued to our CRTs playing Donkey Kong.

It doesn't have to be so — or is History simply going to repeat itself every time some crackpot inventor has a bright idea?

Consider Edison and his light bulb and what it did to candlelight dinners — or Ford and his Model-T and the sexual revolution it created by forcing people out of the hayloft and into the back seat — or Marconi and his "wireless," a device so impersonal you didn't even have to be there to be heard.

The list is endless, but the point is the same. Every time some inveterate tinkerer roars up the basement stairs shouting "Eureka!" the world trembles and the quality of human life diminishes.

Is the advent of the computer

"All right, Miss Whipple. You can buy a word processor."

destined to alter History in the same depersonalized way that the invention of plastic mannequins took the fun out of learning CPR? If things continue the way they are going right now in the midst of the "Technological '80's," the so-called "electronic cottage" is not over the horizon at all; it's already here and we're living in it.

We're all doomed to being nothing more than the thumbs that push the buttons that turn on the machines that rule the world.

How Did It All Begin?

How did a perfectly sane society, evolving according to the precise Laws of Nature, suddenly turn away from our biological heritage to become little more than machines of meat enslaved by micro-chips and the little linear minds that created them?

It wasn't easy.

In the first place, Numbers are not found in Nature. They were discovered much later. In fact, until Noah got the bright idea to "count" everything by "2's," the world ran as smoothly as water off the back of a Unicorn.

When Noah started loading his 90 cubit Love Boat with the beasts of the field, the birds of the air, and the members of his family, things changed. It was no longer good enough to reckon ▷

Shepherds Were the First to Count Things.

things in quantities of "more," "less," and, "that looks about right to me." After Ararat, people began to count. And once that happened, their days were numbered.

Shepherds Were the First to Count Things

Shepherds were the first to fall prey to the insidious compulsion to count things.

The son-in-law in charge of the pair of sheep aboard the Ark went into business the moment the grass turned green. At first he had no trouble keeping track of his fuzzies because Noah had already told him there were "two." So the guy called the big sheep "One," and the smaller sheep "Two," and wandered up to his spring pasture. But lo and behold his surprise to awaken on a bright spring morn "some" months later to find another sheep, albeit a very tiny one, in his flock.

The shepherd had to report the increase in his holdings to Noah, but he didn't want to drag his flock back down the mountain. Moving it once had already created the problem he was currently wrestling with. Who could say what would happen if he moved them again?

The shepherd put his head together and came up with an idea. He folded "Thumb" and "Pinky" into his palm and dipped his remaining fingers into some mud. When he had as many darkened fingers as he did sheep, he hurried to tell Noah what had happened.

"I have more sheep," the shepherd said to Noah, who was busy covering his Ark so nobody could ever find it no matter how many expeditions were sent from *In Search of....*

"How many more?" Noah asked.

"That's just it," the shepherd said. "I don't know. Before you started this thing about counting everything, I'd have said plenty. But now I'm confused." He held up his mud-stained fingers. "There are this many of them up there now, and if I don't hurry and get back to stop them, there's going to be more just as sure as it rains around here."

Noah smiled. "Why, that's 'three,'" he said.

"Three what?" the shepherd asked.

Why, three *sheep*," Noah said.

"But these are *fingers*," the shepherd said.

Noah scratched his beard. "So they are," he said. "Well, then we'll call them digits."

"Why?" the shepherd asked.

"Digits, cubits, who the hell knows why?" Noah said.

Digital Computing Was Created

And so it was that "digital computing" was created, words coined out of the thin air, a practice that would continue to this very day when other, just as meaningless words such as "byte," "nybble," "kluge," "glork," and "grok" clutter the language.

Nothing moved slowly after that. Once things had to be counted, time also speeded up.

The calendar was invented in order to create confusion in people's lives. Prior to it, things were always done on time because there was no time.

Shepherds and everybody else soon ran out of "digits" to count things with. Once you had both hands and both feet blackened, you had to hire help to reckon anything, a practice as expensive then as it is now. Substitute devices were created to count with. ▷

"If you stopped buying all these peripherals, you wouldn't be broke."

Shepherds, always close to nature, began using sheep droppings to keep track of their herds; one drop, one sheep. The result was that shepherds were never invited anywhere. This, by the way, was the first use of a technical device related to a "chip," technology buffalo herders would ultimately perfect.

Strange Twist of History

In a strange twist of History, if the shepherds had been rabbit-herds and had used grains of sand instead of sheep chips, all the sand in the world would have been used up long before the bright boys in "Silicon Valley" started melting the stuff down for their machines and the whole problem brought on by silicon chips would have been avoided. But such are the vagaries of History when Man is allowed to fool around with the Natural Order of things.

Soon everything was being counted. Inventive minds around the globe vied with one another to create more ingenious ways to keep track of things.

For a few centuries it was enough to substitute things for other things, just as the shepherd did with his fingers and later with sheep chips. Usually anything handy would do. A farmer counting his potato crop, for example, might use chickens as counting tokens. A businessman in the button business might use overcoats to tally his accounts.

Obviously, counting in this manner could be cumbersome. By the 19th Century things were growing clearly out of hand, so to speak. Cabbage farmers used candles to keep track of their produce, ship builders used locomotives, shoe salesmen counted with streetcar wheels, and doctors charged patients an arm and a leg, a practice still very much alive.

Something Had to Be Done to Make Calculating Manageable

Something had to be done to make calculating manageable, or the world would clearly soon be buried in "counters." Of course, the manufacture of these counting tokens created lots of jobs,

"I never think of the future. It comes soon enough."
—Einstein

but that was another problem. The problem of too many jobs wouldn't be successfully solved until the 1980's.

Enter the "brilliant" mind of Chuck Babbage, a very sick person who conceived the idea that a machine could be made to count things.

Babbage developed a demoniacal device called the Analytical Engine, named after his sister, Anna Lyt (previously spelled Lit). It was the original kluge and, like the modern day computer it foreshadowed, was destined never to work the way its inventor or operator intended.

Analytical Engines were made smaller and smaller until mini- and micro-engines soon replaced the main-frame originals and could fit in a medium sized office. These small, energy-efficient, one-operator machines used punched cards to count. The cards weren't used as counters, as logic might suggest, however. Rather, *holes* in the cards were meant to stand for things. The insanity of it all should have been clear then, for to use nothing to stand for something makes as much sense as being able to annihilate something twice.

No longer were shirt-sleeved, green-visored accountants accountable for counting anything (poetic justice, that), because the *responsibility* was taken from people and *turned over to machines* which had *no souls, hearts,* or any ability at all to do anything with a spindled, torn or mutilated card.

Once the transition from men to machines was made, the way ▷

Tomorrow and tomorrow and tomorrow...

Futurism is flourishing. Computers are now able to project what will happen days, weeks, months and even years ahead.

Because computers leave so little to the imagination with their precise prognostications, the world of tomorrow is becoming a reality today.

To make certain nobody is left behind in the rush for tomorrow, CompuFear, a software firm, has developed a program that predicts everything that will happen for months in advance.

Nobody has to sit back and idly spin out their lives in peaceful day to day wondering about what lies over the hill. The terror of tomorrow can be theirs now for only a few bucks and a few minutes at their terminals.

An official of CompuFear has this to say about the accuracy of their program, which is based on current world affairs: "Please pay in advance."

TEN THINGS TO REMEMBER WHEN THE URGE TO ENTER A COMPUTER STORE STRIKES

1. You can't think of a single intelligent question to ask.

2. The salesman has 3 unintelligible answers for each of your stupid questions.

3. Computers and electric chairs both run on electricity.

4. You've never needed to know more than 2 or 3 things at once before, so why should you now?

5. If you are over 21, most people who understand computers are younger than you.

6. Computer technology is predicated on the inference that there is more intelligence in a grain of sand than in your head.

7. The premise may be right.

8. It's cheaper in the long run to take a cold shower.

9. Whatever you buy will end up in your kid's room anyway.

10. Maybe they're only a fad.

was open for a complete breakdown of the Natural Order. Management made its move. A small corporation in New Jersey, International Babbage Machines quickly developed the white shirt and tie, slipped men with short hair inside them, and the rest is history (with a small *h*). Marketing replaced Humanity. The end had already arrived, but ordinary people spinning ordinary lives were too naive in those early, trusting years when a briefcase, a short haircut, and a corporate image still meant something.

Once International Babbage Machines got its foot in the collective office door, others quickly followed suit. Dozens of huge corporations with their own ideas of how to hasten the downfall of civilization by technological refinements geared up for the final assault.

American Telephone and Take-itall, the "wrong number giant," put its gnomes to work building a Babbage machine that would fit on the head of a pin. Finding the pins was easy, but the smallest creature on earth couldn't produce a chip small enough. ▷

"Mark my words, those video games are going to ruin their homework."

ON POETRY AND THE COMPUTER

Wrought by Man:

PIPPA'S SONG
The year's at the spring
And day's at the morn;
Morning's at seven;
The hill-side's dew-pearl'd;
The lark's on the wing;
The snail's on the thorn:
God's in His heaven —
All's right with the world!
—Robert Browning

Wrought by computer:

0100 10101 1010001 01010101
01001 01010 1010101 0101010
001 1010 101010 101 0101 101
101010 001 1010 011010 10 01
10000110 101001 0100 00100
001000 001010 10 0100 00100
101010 01 0110 0100 10101 10
01110 0110 01010 111000 111
01101 01011101 110110 1010 0
10101 101001 1010101 101110
—(All's not right with the world!)

The Breakthrough

Then came the breakthrough. Michael Roe, frustrated from counting with drawers full of sand grains as counters, condensed a number of grains into a tiny packet or *sand*wich, stuck some wires into it and, *voilà,* the transistor (an acronym formed from *tran* and *sistor*) was born. The device, later refined even smaller so that twenty-seven trillion of them could fit inside a budget director's heart, was named in the inventor's honor, the Mike Roe Chip.

The floodgates of change were opened. The micro-miniaturization of Babbage machines made it possible to produce tiny, tiny things.

The military saw the advantage of smallness for it fit directly into their philosophy of short-sightedness. They began to produce smaller and smaller minds to fit the even smaller heads the new technology produced. Soon these marvels of miniaturization began producing ideas which were so small it took an entire general staff to see one and a whole Pentagon to get it in motion.

The military strategist's dream, computerized armies that would allow generals to direct entire wars from the safety of deep pits in the ground with nothing more than a joy stock and an Apple II, was realized.

And so it has come to be that the future of the earth has been reduced to nothing more than a global video game waiting for someone to play the first quarter.

A really dumb idea, counting things, has been perverted into the Technological Revolution and has given us the answer to the question, When will it all end?

Computers shouldn't rule the world. People should rule the world.

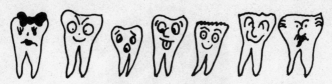

CompuDent

The fully automated, computerized dentist's office is on the way. Already a gadget junkie's paradise, the computerized office will let the dentist get rid of the one remaining thing in the office that makes his work so utterly boring, himself.

The patient's visit will be completely controlled by a computer. The door will open automatically, flashing lights will show the patient to the chair, which will adjust itself precisely to his or her anatomy, and a robotic dental arm will drop out of the ceiling, ready to go to work, its progress checked every step of the way against computerized records which are kept in CentroDent, a mainframe computer in Evanston.

To keep the visit from being overly depersonalized by the computer and its slaved machines, a synthesized dentist's voice will soothe the patient with words of comfort, understanding, and that old stand-by, dentist's humor.

Herewith, a recording of an experimental visit to a computerized dentist's office:

Dr. CompuDent: *Good morning or afternoon. Please have a seat in the waiting room. Your appointment will be delayed because we've had an emergency. Mr. Coffee will be happy if you said hello. If you are a little person, hi there, how are you, I am fine, would you like a piece of sugarless gum while you're waiting?*

An hour and a half later.

Dr. CompuDent: *Please enter the door with the flashing light. Sit in the chair. Lean back. Open your mouth. This isn't going to hurt a bit. Wider please while I put this suction pipe, 27 cotton cylinders and a television camera in your mouth. What do you think of the crisis in the Mideast, the economy, and the Democratic presidential candidates? Wider please. Do you want Novocain? Answer in one second or I'll proceed raw. Wider please. This isn't going to hurt a bit.*
Patient: AAAAGGGHHHH!!!!

ARE COMPUTERS ALIENS FROM OUTER SPACE?

Their Origin Is a Mystery

The advent of computers is unmatched in all of recorded History. Never before has such sophisticated technology appeared in so many places so quickly — and been adapted into use so unquestioningly — as that of computers.

Technologically speaking, Planet Earth is unusually slow to develop and adapt new, innovative methods of artificial evolution. Consider, for example, the horse.

It is universally agreed by horstorians that the horse came into general usage in the 3rd Century B.C. (Before the Cart) and paralleled the development of the wheel.

In pre-horstoric times, horses were made of clay or bronze or were carved out of big chunks of marble ("Chip away everything that doesn't look like a horse and there you have it"). Virtually every culture around the globe, no matter how primitive, had prototypes of the horse, some of them statuesque. Models of horse designs from these early cultures are still on view in museums and town squares. They are remarkably similar to those which were later made of meat, though they didn't work as well.

Rolf di Lorryen

In O B.C. a daringly stupid entrepreneur named Rolf, an engineer by trade and determined to make a fortune for himself, decided to invent the cart. Putting the cart before the horse is but ▷

"We tried computers, but there's still nothing like old-fashioned teacher rapport to hold their attention."

a single example of one man's perverse brilliance. His other was to invent the truck or "lorry" which he planned to use to haul coke, which he thought would hasten breadmaking. However, Rolf of the Lorryin' as he was called, or Rolf di Lorryen, was ahead of his time. There was still nothing to pull the cart.

Enter Victor Carousel, a French thrill-ride enthusiast, who, to make something of a preposterous story easy to swallow, molded hamburger into horseflesh.

By the mid-1600's horses were popular all over the world. By the end of the 19th Century they were filling the streets, which led to the invention of acid-resistant Totes.

The point is, it took over 1000 years including weekends and holidays for the horse to become a household word, e.g. "horse" feathers, "horse" d'oeuvres, "horse" of a different color, "horse" 'n pfeffer, "Horse" Wessel, "horse" radish, and those iniquitous places of ill repute, the "horse" house.

Consider then the remarkable, inexplicable, instantaneous and universal appearance of the computer.

There Are No Computers in Ancient Writings

You'll find no computers in Egyptian hieroglyphics. There are no stone computers on Easter Island. Nobody ever said, "My kingdom for a computer." No primitive tribes worshipped computers, even though some witch doctors are said to have read the future in goat chips. No early civilizations made tiny clay computers which would eventually be copied and sold to tourists from roadside stands.

The fact is indisputable. *There is absolutely no historical record of computers existing before 1946!* Doesn't that tell us something? You bet.

In 1946, Joe Fabitz of Eustace, Oregon, saw a flight of "strange silvery birds flying ten thousand million miles an hour" over Mount Shasta (*N.Y. Times,* May 6, 1946, Believe It or Don't Page). Later, in what can only be described as a frenzy of bird sightings, countless others reported similar observations of identical flights of these "strange silvery birds."

Of course, we know now that those "birds" weren't any of our ▷

Computer Dysfunction

There may be a cure for computers on the horizon. Science has discovered a 20th-Century malady that may be just the disease we need to save us from computerism. It is **Computer Dysfunction.**

Computer Dysfunction is a person's inability to use a computer through fear, ignorance or poor eye-hand coordination. It is a clearly defined disease for which there is no known cure.

Unfortunately, it is not yet known how Computer Dysfunction is spread. Until computer haters learn how to transmit disease, the epidemic of computers will continue to affect the nation. It's suspected that the malady may be spread by a byte from a computer bug. Others believe computerism is a venal disease spread by prolonged contact with computer salesmen.

Hope lies with continued research. Computer haters are asked to send their contributions for Computer Dysfunction Spread to the March of Dymes.

tiny feathered friends at all. They were *aliens from outer space — flying saucers!*

It certainly doesn't take a so-called "computer expert" to figure out the connection.

Computers were introduced onto the planet in 1946 aboard flying saucers. They are aliens!

How Did Computer Aliens Go Undetected for So Long?

Good question.

The first of the invading computers escaped detection because *they looked just like people!*

Wherever these ubiquitous invaders have come from, the devious creatures who devised them and sent them to our planet made the mistake of making them resemble us. They didn't know that nobody on earth is impressed by people. Earthlings are impressed by machines.

"It's the down payment on the peripherals he needed."

In the mid-'50's another invasion from space was tried. This time computers were made to look like automobiles. The intelligence behind the machines was beginning to catch on. Loaded with tons of chrome and weighing up to 'leventy thousand pounds, the machines nearly succeeded in accomplishing the goal of those who sent them by killing people in droves (drives?).

But the planned invasion of Earth and the complete takeover of the planet could not be effected until the aliens held positions of great power. Nobody would elect a '56 Chevy president. The invasion was stalemated. It was clear to the aliens that surrogates would not do. They would have to come here themselves.

The breakthrough came in the 1970's when the aliens quit trying to fool us and invaded in uncountable numbers. Not only did they come themselves, but they brought entire population centers with them.

The alien cities, extremely small by Earth standards, began to show up everywhere. In fact, they were so tiny they could be hidden anywhere.

Soon the miniature micro-cities had infiltrated every machine made on Earth. And the aliens knew it was the machines that commanded respect. They were *in*.

The micro-cits, later shortened to simply, chips, each containing an alien population of hundreds of millions, could be found in refrigerators, space-craft, automobiles, wristwatches, nuclear missiles, barberpoles, cameras, hair dryers and thousands of other essential products. There, deep within the guidance systems of the machines that rule the world, the tiny chip people go about their business — making decisions for us.

As hard as it may be for some to accept, there is no decision in their lives, no matter how large or small, that is not a direct order from the Chip People.

Where Will It All End?

Good question.

It may already be too late. Even now the decisions for peace or war, who lives and who dies, who pays taxes and who gets away without, who will get your telephone bill while you get theirs, and millions of others are being made daily by the Chip People.

Computer anarchy is just around the corner.

How Do We Stop Them?

Good question.

The answer is to let them know you know. Don't be fooled by your watch or radio alarm, the carburetor in your car, your beer cooler, barberpole, MX missile, video game, or Pacemaker. Let the little s.o.b.'s know you know they're in there.

Tell them you know. Open up your watch, your refrigerator, your hair dryer and barberpole and shout at the top of your lungs, "I'm mad as hell and I'm not going to take orders from you anymore."

It's not too late to stop computers from taking over the Earth. Send the little alien bastards back to where they came from. Make a few decisions on your own for a change.

Let's hear it. All together now, Earth for Earthlings! ▣

The unfortunate thing about computerholics is that they refuse to be anonymous.

Who's Really in Charge Here?

TALKING COMPUTERS

They Don't Really

Anyone who has heard "synthesized" speech from a computer realizes what a marvelous thing the human voice is, even one from Brooklyn or Mississippi. They may all sound different, but at least you can understand them.

Not so with "synthesized" speech. These simple examples prove the point.

Sample of human speech-
"Hi there. I'm Fred, your new neighbor. Mind if I bring a few friends over to use your pool on the Fourth of July?"

This speech is clear, intelligible and very much to the point. Human speech gives the listener the opportunity to make an intelligent decision instead of just nodding dumbly because he didn't understand the question.

Sample of computer speech-
"hEIlOoooO tHIsSSisSS yOOourRRr LlifFe sSSupPPooOrrTtTT ssSyYsSStTeMMm dOoo yYooOU wAannNtT MmoOrRre OxXy-shielsStckdBz OorRR ayy bBloooDd tRnsdliexfhisSDBiX? AanNsSWerR iNn OnnNe sSsEconNNd Orr Ii WilLL pPulL yoOuRr pPluUgGg.

Computer speech not only requires excellent hearing, but rather quick reaction time as well.

WHAT IF...
Famous People and Events of History Had Computers?

The lesson of History is that we never get anything right the first time. The corollary is that we get the chance to keep on trying.

Computers and their insidious penchant for perfection change all that. With computers, everything is done exactly "right" the first time.

Imagine, then, if the greatest figures and events of history had been computerized...just as History from now on is doomed to be.

The Creation —

If God had used an Apple instead of letting Adam and Eve get their hands on one, the Creation could have been completed in a mere 2.75 days. This would have provided God with 4.25 days of rest during which time he could have reconsidered the whole project and dumped it in favor of creating Ork,which had the advantage of cancellation built in.

The Garden of Eden—

If God's Apple had come from California instead of a tree, Adam would have been so preoccupied dinking around with it he would never have noticed Eve's nakedness. She would have become so annoyed living with the world's first hacker she would have divorced him...*before* there were any children.

The Flood—

Noah could have converted cubits to inches and feet and finished in half the time,thereby allowing him to spend more time with the passenger list. He could have left off a few marginal creatures such as cockroaches and computer salesmen, and included others such as Unicorns and intelligible sportscasters.

The Plagues—

Magazine subscription renewal

reminders mailed every three weeks *ad infinitum* would have proved a much better scourge than frogs.

The Exodus—

No tribes would have been lost had they kept in touch on a computer network. The result would have been a much larger, more effective garment industry.

The X Commandments—

With WordStar, Moses's revisions of his first draft would have been word perfect, with no spelling errors, justified right and left margins, with automatic pagination, and he'd have had no blisters from wielding a hammer and chisel.

Attila the Hun—

The confusion which resulted in duplicate raids because none of his hordes could tell one round eye encampment from another would have been eliminated if software for *Village Pillage* had been available.

The Dark Ages—

Eyestrain and writer's cramp would have been a thing of the past for monks copying illuminated manuscripts if they'd had word processors. A drawback, however, would have been that the Enlightenment would have arrived sooner, hastening the series of "Revolutions" which have led to the Electronic Revolution which is the Beginning of the End.

Marco Polo—

With computerized communications networks and navigation satellites, Polo's journeys would have been so short they wouldn't have inspired a TV mini-series, thereby freeing all those evenings watching it for more useful pastimes like thinking or humming.

Columbus' Discovery of America—

If computerized records had been kept of all the previous visits in the first place, there would have been no need for Columbus to repeat the trip. The Indians would still be living in peace, the last people on earth who had a crack at it.

Also, with computers on board the Nina, Pinta and Santa Maria, the ships could have made a simple "fly-by" instead of landing to eventually learn that Miami was not the East Indies and the only riches it would ever produce would be furs and pink Cadillacs, neither of which were of any value to Ferdinand and Isabella, or anybody else of good taste. ▷

The Charge of the Light Brigade—

A computer print-out of the enemy's defenses might have inspired a charge of the *Heavy* Brigade into the Valley of Death instead, changing the battle's outcome, shortening the Crimean War, thereby eliminating the need for Florence Nightingale's services, thus leaving no inspiration for the Red Cross and with it the inexplicable presence of coffee and donuts at floods, fires and other natural disasters.

Descartes—

The simplest of word processing programs would have allowed Descartes to run through all the permutations and combinations of *I, think, therefore,* and, *am* rather than settling on the first one that came to his mind. Once the futility of trying to encapsulate the basis for personal reality with Reason was realized, speculative philosophy would have come to a dead end, eliminating Existentialist arguments as excuses for war, and leaving men to hoe their gardens.

Early Egyptian kids played Dungeon Draggin' without computers.

It was tough getting a deck chair on the Ark without computerized boarding passes.

The American Revolution—

The whole mess might not have begun if the tax bills which triggered it had been mailed by an impersonal computer somewhere in King George's basement. With nobody to argue with but a machine, the Colonists would have eventually grown so frustrated writing letters that were ignored they'd have paid the bills just to end the rain of paper addressed to, "Dear Mr. and Mrs. Colonist, Your tax bill is due, Mr. and Mrs. Colonist and so, Mr. and Mrs. Colonist, if you..."

Lincoln's Gettysburg Address—

Nobody would have been moved by anyone, even Honest Abe, intoning a nine-digit zip code.

World Wars I, II, III et al—

Even a 6-year-old General with a TRS-80 and VisiCalc would see that the bottom line in the war business does not justify the start-up costs.

The Future—

With the computers that are already here today, what will happen tomorrow is calculated and printed out before it happens, eliminating the need for Tomorrow in the first place...and so ending everything Yesterday. 🖥

**A programmer, left, demonstrates proper keyboard stance
for a computer science major.**

COMPUTER PERSONAE

TO KNOW THEM IS TO AVOID THEM

Chapter Two

THE HACKER

What It Is and How to Spot Him

There is no accurate record of when the first hacker was born. Some believe hackers evolved from simpler forms of life such as newts, salamanders, and bottom dwelling slugs, in the traditional Darwinian scheme. Others, more charitable, perhaps, suspect the hacker emerged fully developed from totally unrelated life forms, meaning space dust, Extra Terrestrials (E.T., Pod People, etc.) and math teachers. Whichever the case may eventually prove to be, there is complete agreement that the hacker is unique among creatures.

True Hackers Began to Appear in the '50's and '60's

True hackers began to appear on college campuses in the late '50's and early '60's. An earlier version of the same sub-specie, the "slip-stick wizard," usually an engineering student or math major, was common at that time. It was difficult to distinguish hackers from these simpler types. Not only did they look alike in white shirts and jeans belted midway up the chest with cuffs that exposed 6-8 inches of white sock and ankle, but they also had similar mind-sets; everything had a place, a number, and a sequence. Hackers blended in with the slip-sticks, who didn't blend in anywhere.

Computers Were Untamed Monsters

In those early days of hacking, computers were untamed monsters which filled rooms and could brown out a city with their energy needs. They generated more heat than light and required huge air-conditioners to cool them. A bit of spin-off technology the rest of the world has learned to endure are those very same air-conditioners which have now been installed in movie theatres and department stores which can cool a 178-pound piece of meat to 32° before the feature begins.

Because the machinery of computing was so complex and subject to constant breakdowns, the first hackers spent as much time

---

10 FAVORITE HACKER VACATION SPOTS

1. Silicon Valley
2. Computerland
3. Howard Johnson's Motel, Cupertino, CA
4. Computer Science Lab, M.I.T.
5. Dr. Zap's Video Arcade
6. Radio Shack Computer Center
7. Plato's Cave
8. EPCOT Center
9. TRON Festival
10. Up in room

repairing their machines as dinking with them.

Hackerism Spread Like a Plague

It wasn't until the advent of the mini- and later, micro-computers, developed out of the urgent need to pack more mega-tonnage into tinier missiles and other humanitarian pursuits, that hackerism as we know it today spread like a selective plague.

The minis and micros had the advantage of minimal size and maximum power combined with multi-user adaptability. The huge kluges of the '50's spent most of their up time under the iron-handed guidance of the scientists and engineers who developed and built them. They were generally under the control of those who paid their salaries, Big Business and its parent company, Big Government.

Nerds Came Out of the Closet

With new machines that took up but a small corner of a subterreanean room and drew no more power than a Lionel train set, the groundwork was laid for fullscale hacking. Nerds who would have otherwise been left in the attics of social change were finding places that would accept them. They came out of the closet, only to disappear into the basement.

The Information Revolution

When Man first appeared on the face of the earth and lifted his wondering eyes to the sacred vault of the heavens filled with countless stars which overwhelmed him and made him feel small, what manner of questions raced through his mind?

Did he ask himself, "I wonder how many clutch pedals are in inventory?" or "What was the average annual precipitation over the last hundred years in Zambia?" or "What is the megatonnage needed to crisp-fry everyone else like me ten times over?" No, that first inquisitive, wondering guy didn't ask dumb things like that. He asked himself, "Who am I?" "What am I doing here?" "Where am I going?"

Ask a computer how many clutch pedals you've got in inventory and it'll tell you. But ask it who you are and it'll reveal just how vacuous the information revolution really is.

The Ultimate Mind Trip

Hacking became the total introvert's ultimate mind trip. Unfettered by social pressures and rules, he could let his gray matter hang out with his hair in front of a machine which did exactly what he told it to do, no more and no less (usually). ▷

Fueled by Coca-Cola, coffee and Chinese food, the hacker had found his heaven.

Hackers Were Privy to the Secrets of the Ages

Computer mutants could write their own rules. And they did. The results were programs, most of which dealt with world domination, subjugation and mastery. These guys didn't mess around with the need to work their way to the top like other megalomaniacs; they started at the top. And, as the ultimate masters of the mystery of the new technology, hackers were privy to the secrets of the ages and used them to stay on top.

The real world, that random event dice game rolled by nobody, was a terrifying place to be compared to the hyper-space of the totally controlled, programmed and pre-planned world within a world within a machine within a basement within a university.

Alarm!

Had it stayed that way, had the hackers stayed in their burrows playing World Dominator, they might have been ignored. But, alarm! All hackers are not in

"It keeps my mind sharp for writing manuals."

their basement lairs and all hacking isn't done late at night when the normal world is sleeping.

The hacker has come out of his electronic cage and walks among us, stalking us, looking coolly down his waxen nose which has never felt the scorch of the sun through tiny, beady, red night eyes, quietly scoffing up his ragged sleeve at the daylight drones who make the world go round. And he believes he alone has seen the vision of Ultimate Truth and that he alone quests for it.

What Is His Vision

And what is his vision, this noble goal to which the hacker is so earnestly dedicated? What is the real objective of his consuming ambition to master the machines he believes will master the world? To score. To score big. To make the ultimate buck. To knock down a million before he's twenty, surely before he's thirty. By fair means or foul, by perverse programming or unkeying the code to a corporation's millions, he's going to get his.

In other words, the hacker is no different from those he spurns ...but he's so seduced by his machine mentality, he believes he is.

Pity the Poor Hacker

So pity the poor hacker. He be-

lieves he controls the machine. But the truth is that *he who really controls the machine is the one who never turns the goddamned thing on.*

"My brother's in computer programming."

CompuShrink

The ultimate in computerized medicine, self - analysis through your own computer is now available on a program called Psych-Out.

The patient lies down on a couch in the privacy of his or her own home. The program is booted into the patient's own computer.

The patient then talks to the computer for 55 minutes while the computer plays tic-tac-toe, hums, and nods off, interrupting with occasional "Hmms," "Interestings," and "Would you like to tell me mores?"

PsychOut is priced just out of the reach of everyone.

A DAY IN THE LIFE OF A HACKER

*From Boredom to Ennui
and Back*

Hackers live for hacking. A study of garage sales in neighborhoods where hackers abound invariably turns up terrific bargains in golf clubs, scuba gear, tennis racquets, skis, sailboats, surfboards, hang gliders, aerobatic airplanes, pressurized EVA suits, and even Scrabble games. Why? Because hackers forsake everything for their passion, which is to sit in front of a flickering screen and tap out inanities into a machine.

A day in the life of a typical hacker is as exciting as waiting for a bonsai tree to mature or listening to Lawrence Welk records at 7 AM or watching a hacker watching a hacker watching a CRT. Even Howard Cosell broadcasting a chess game *with* facial expression causes the heart to beat faster than a hacker punching the HELP button will.

Hackers don't sleep, even if to look at one suggests he is sleeping. The dishevelment of his clothes and two to three days' growth of stubble may make it appear that he's been sleeping, but he hasn't. His day is 24 hours of thinking about computers or diddling with them.

Hackers reluctantly emerge into the real world just in time to catch the morning rush. They somnambulently muddle through the day at their office, garage, classroom, store or operating room, robotically doing what they must to stay on the payroll, but always their minds are on their machine which lurks like a temptress in the corner of the den or garage turned into a computer center, waiting for him to return home and caress it with his willing finger.

Lunch time for hackers is spent at computer stores or in front of racks of computer magazines. Often in the company of others with the same addiction, sometimes alone, the hacker touches the machines he'll one day own, or reads about them in articles written by other hackers with word processors.

There are the evening hours which alert a hacker to his real *raison d'être,* for when he's safely back home in the sterile cloister which is his haven from family dog, kids, and wife, he can do what he's been waiting for all day long. To hack.

From 6 in the evening until the sun rises as it must, the hacker sits at his terminal, staring, wondering, punching, diddling, tweaking, twiddling and otherwise relating to a machine full of invisible pips of electricity and nothing else.

No wonder he's got rid of his squash racquet and running shoes and let his subscription to *Adventure* magazine lapse. What's the point of all that stuff when the world outside has ceased to exist?

A HACKER'S PHOTO ALBUM

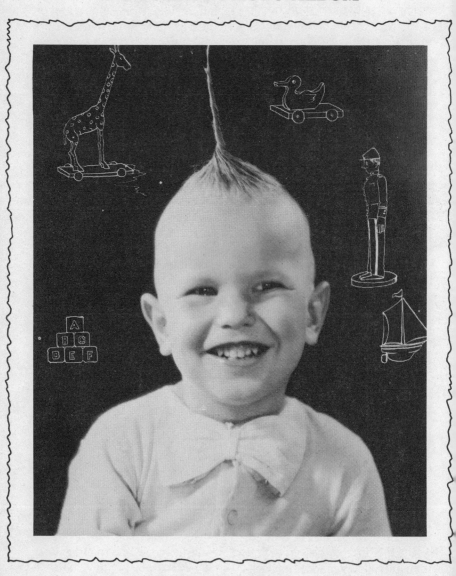

The genetic results of Hackerism in offspring.
Definitely not a pretty sight.

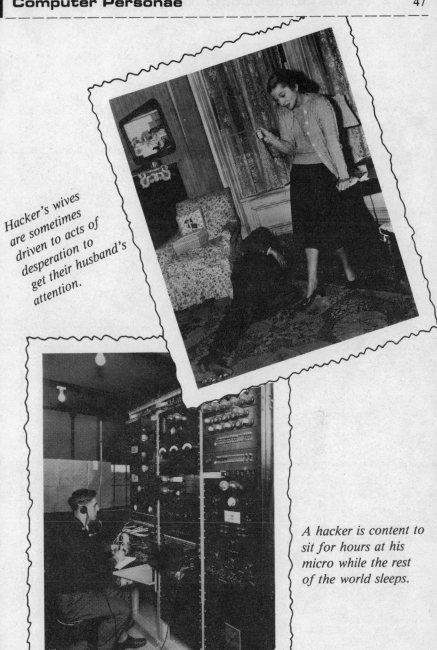

Hacker's wives are sometimes driven to acts of desperation to get their husband's attention.

A hacker is content to sit for hours at his micro while the rest of the world sleeps.

There's nothing more exciting to a hacker than looking for bugs in his program tapes.

Even the entreaties of a beautiful girl can't pull a confirmed hacker away from the only love in his life, his "kluge."

Hackerism and the megalomania associated with the disease frequently causes their brains to grow too big for their heads.

THE ANATOMY OF A HACKER

Ménage à deux

There is no single hacker profile, and that's what makes them dangerous. It's possible for a hacker to mingle with ordinary society and go undetected for long periods of time, as long as he doesn't open his mouth.

Here are the most common hacker traits and characteristics to look for if you suspect a hacker has slipped into your life. Watch for them. Be on your guard. If someone you know or love begins to exhibit these signs, it's probably already too late. Once someone has turned to a computer for companionship, affection and emotional support you might as well find a replacement. He'll never come back.

The Hacker:

1. Has a steel-trap mind
2. Is very bright
3. Is an overachiever
4. Gets good to excellent grades
5. Cannot accept failure
6. Can be dangerously devious
7. Lives like a hermit
8. Capable of committing the "perfect crime"
9. Is a direct descendent of the slide rule wizard
10. Half man, half machine
11. Can multiply large numbers in his head
12. Is a master of logical mysteries
13. Believes he is privy to the secrets of the ages
14. Subliminally suggests he knows something you don't and never will
15. Often looks like a dropout from Woodstock generation
16. Demands a high salary and believes he is worth more
17. Can be a consummate team player
18. Needs no sleep
19. Subsists on very little food
20. Smells mildly of Szechuan Chinese food
21. His primary interaction on planet is with his computer
22. Has pockets full of pencils
23. May not shave yet
24. Knows what all those little buttons on a calculator do
25. Is the ultimate introvert
26. Loves complex situations
27. Logic dominates his mind and life
28. Has a delightful, rather puckish sense of humor
29. Views the world as a machine
30. Believes no problem is too complex
31. Knows he can solve any problem
32. Convinced security systems were designed for him to foil
33. Lives for the challenge of computing
34. Schoolwork, homework and intellectual tasks don't phase him
35. Loves to crash computers for the fun of it
36. Believes he's on earth to find bugs and kill them dead
37. Entertains vast fantasies of omnipotence
38. Delights in his megalomania
39. Loves being seduced by a machine or logic problem
40. Believes that the real function of computers is play

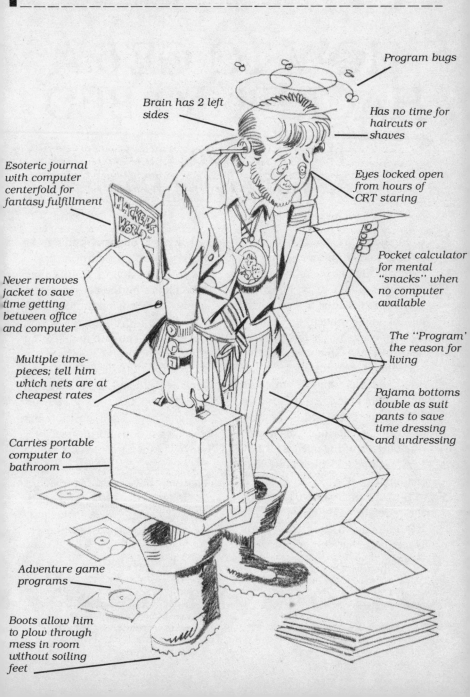

Program bugs

Brain has 2 left sides

Has no time for haircuts or shaves

Esoteric journal with computer centerfold for fantasy fulfillment

Eyes locked open from hours of CRT staring

Never removes jacket to save time getting between office and computer

Pocket calculator for mental "snacks" when no computer available

The "Program" the reason for living

Multiple time-pieces; tell him which nets are at cheapest rates

Pajama bottoms double as suit pants to save time dressing and undressing

Carries portable computer to bathroom

Adventure game programs

Boots allow him to plow through mess in room without soiling feet

HOW TO GET A HACKER TO BED

What to Do When the Chips Are Down

Computers are destroying the nuclear family. Junior spends all his spare time at the arcade playing video games or in his room playing with knobs or even reading manuals under the covers with a flashlight. Sis has been seduced by the silicon syndrome and does her homework on her boyfriend's terminal. Mom pecks out her shopping list on her own kitchen computer and dad hasn't been out of his den for weeks. The nucleus of the nuclear family is a machine and the family is in shambles.

But the final straw, the thing that's really ungluing what little left remains to hold the family together is that the computer is replacing sex.

Hackers, never known as heavyweights of bedroom prowess or perversion, are more than ever falling by the bedside, leaving behind them a nation of frustrated women. Husbands and boyfriends who are hooked on the mass opiate of computerism have turned off their libidos and replaced them with LIFO's, LILO's and LOGO's. Bawd has become baud. Bed position has given way to bit position. A bio-sensor has a whole new meaning that can't be found in an anatomy book, and blowback is no longer what you think. Nobody snickers when somebody mentions getting skewed and *nobody* laughs when a friend's joystick is down because these are

A computer can do a lot, but it still can't scratch you where it itches.

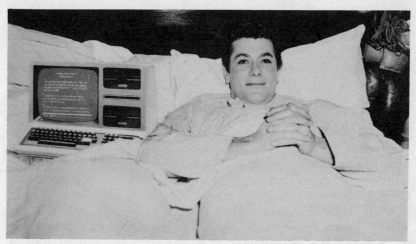

A wife's dramatic face-lift (left) changed her hacker husband into a tyger, though smoking a cigarette after is still a problem.

serious matters to hackers.

What's a woman to do?

The tragedy is that it is men who have become hackers while their wives and girl friends turn to pulp romances, *People* magazine, and Phil Donahue for vicarious sex. As stimulating as watching an interview with an avowed shoe fetishist might be, it will rarely cause the earth to move for her.

The problem is that a hacker is perfectly content to tweak plastic knobs while getting eyestrain in a cramped den or closet watching a flickering CRT while the woman who used to be in his life flips her own knobs on the bedroom TV.

The solution is to attack the problem on its own terms. There is a way to turn on the turned-off hacker and save the American way of bedroom life. How?

By talking to the hacker in a language he understands. Use the words he cares about. Whisper them softly in his ear. Dress in clothes that naturally excite a ▷

hacker. Leave the filmy gowns in the drawer and parade around the room in the things he associates with a good time. Prepare exotic food for him, the kind that only a hacker can eat. And above all, read to him.

For those who are too shy to ask their family physician or even their best girl friend for the names of things that will get her hacker back in the sack, here's the approved list:

Phrases That Will Turn Him On—

"How about a little time sharing?"

"Would you like to try a manual entry?"

"My response time is shorter than an ELF."

"I run on AC or DC."

"I'll trade you my software for your hardware."

"I'm a member of Aslib."

"Want to try my back-up equipment?"

"How about a digital search?"

"Boot my system."

"I need my cards punched."

"Mind if I run a cylinder scan on you?"

"Wanna see my dedicated port?"

"You can have direct access if you want."

"How about a flip-flop?"

"Are you interested in gang-punching?"

"Like to see my head rotor?"

"Let me try your joystick."

"KISS my system."

"You'll always be LILO in my system."

"It's time to log in."

"Massage my input."

"Wanna twiddle my mouse?"

"I've also got a slow mode."

"I'm programmed for parallel processing."

"I'm into RAM."

"Let's advance the state of the art."

"Like some digital timesharing of my TTS?"

Bernard Shaw on video games — "Life would be tolerable but for its amusements."

Clothes That Will Drive Him Mad —

White shirt with plastic pencil case in pocket

T-shirt with rock group on front

White socks

Worn out running shoes

Shiny suit pants

Hawaiian shirt

12-pound wingtips

Carry a briefcase

Food To Stimulate Him —

Warm Coke

Twinkies

Szechuan food

Week-old pizza

Oreo cookies

Lukewarm coffee

Selected Readings To Whisper in His Ear —

On circuit operation (Read as if lecturing):

The input signal is impressed on the grid of the voltage amplifier tube, T_1. This signal is amplified and appears across R_{g1} after experiencing a 180° phase shift.

On common polyphase rectifier circuits:

A three-phase delta-wye circuit, sometimes known as a three-phase, half-wave rectifier circuit, has the disadvantage of giving a large ripple voltage in the output circuit.

If all else fails, try this winning line:

This last line is sure to get him aroused.

$$I = \frac{E}{X_T} \text{ where } X_T = X_{c1} +$$

$$\frac{X_{C2}X_{C3}}{X_{c2} + X_{c3}} + \frac{X_{C4}X_{C5}X_{C6}}{X_{c4}X_{c5} + X_{c7}} + (2+2=5)$$

Computing = Confusion

If God had meant for Man to compute, He would have given him 10,000 fingers.

101 THINGS TO DO WITH A DEAD COMPUTER

It's hard enough to come up with uses for a computer that works, but what do you do with one that doesn't?

1. Use it as a milking stool.

2. Keep goldfish in it.

3. Use it as a mirror.

4. Store cookies in it.

5. Upholster it for a pillow.

6. Use it as a highway cone.

7. Use it for target practice.

8. Anchor your boat with it.

9. Block up your car on it.

10. Keep your socks in it.

11. Collect pocket lint in it.

12. Mail it to an enemy.

13. Let your Chihuahua live in it.

14. Raise bees in it.

15. Use it as an ant farm.

16. Use it as an ant trap.

17. Rent it as a roach motel.

18. Block a wobbly table leg with it.

19. Steam vegetables in it.

20. Block hats on it.

21. Store your wig on it.

22. Talk to it when you don't want an argument.

23. Keep jellybeans in it.

24. Use it as a pencil holder.

25. Lure an E.T. out of the woods with it.

26. Sit on it.

27. Use it as a footstool.

28. Put in on porch as a milk box.

29. Wear it as a broach.

30. Use it as a hibachi.

31. Use it as a trash basket.

32. Plant flowers in it.

33. Raise mushrooms in it.

34. Throw it at a howling cat.

35. Fill it with kitty litter and let the cat use it.

36. Give it a funeral.

37. Place on a pedestal as sculpture.

38. Fill with birdseed and hang in a tree.

39. Bronze and place on mantel.

40. Put into orbit.

41. Drop out 2nd floor window onto door-to-door salesman.

42 Keep recipes in it.

43. Use it as a bird house.

44. Store buttons in it.

45. Pop popcorn in it.

46. Burn incense in it.

47. Take it for a walk on a leash.

48. Leave it on a park bench.

49. Use it as a mailbox.

50. Put wheels on it and use it for a shopping cart.

51. Keep your pipes in it.

52. Use it as a magazine rack.

53. Use it as a doorstop.

54. Use it as a breadbox.

55. Keep loose change in it.

56. Keep dead letters in it.

57. Use it as a gerbil cage.

58. Keep your string collection in it.

59. Burn kerosene in it for portable heat.

60. Enter it in a Trash-of-the-Month contest.

61. Bowl with it.

62. Blast it into orbit.

63. Use it as a soap dish.

64. Wear it as a diving helmet.

65. Sell it to aborigines as an idol.

66. Put a handle on it and drive pilings with it. ▷

67. Get another and have two of them.

68. Fill it with ice and use as a beer cooler.

69. Hang it on the wall as a sconce.

70. Hang it from the ceiling as a mobile.

71. Convince a Pole it still works.

72. Keep a canary in it.

73. Shrink it and have it set in a ring.

74. Expand it and live in it.

75. Engrave it and use it as a headstone.

76. Send it back to Silicon Valley, collect.

77. Use it as a lobster trap.

78. Moor your boat to it.

79. Sell it to the Pentagon, where it'll become surplus anyway.

80. Mix ice tea in it.

81. Use it for batting practice.

82. Paint stripes on it and give it to your barber.

83. Use the parts to start your own computer company.

84. Sell it to the Japanese as new technology.

85. Give it to Secretary Watt to dispose of in a Federal Landfill Park.

86. Use it as a test-track pylon.

87. Use it as a hood ornament.

88. Wallpaper over it.

89. Put cast iron antlers on it and give it to an Italian for his yard.

90. Put it in the collection plate on Sunday.

91. Open it up as a tiny roadside stand.

92. Use it as a mausoleum for gnomes.

93. Use it as a butcher block.

94. Send it marked "Fragile" through the U.S. Postal System.

95. Leave it on your car seat with the door unlocked.

96. Use it as an umbrella stand.

97. Get off a bus one stop before it does.

98. Tell your friends you have a microwave oven.

99. Bury Fido in it.

100. Frost it and enter it in a cake contest.

And if you really want to get rid of it

101. Try fixing it yourself

COMPUTER KITS

Let the Builder Beware

There is a breed of masochists known as kit builders who proudly point to their refrigerator, their television set, the swimming-pool-size satellite antenna in their backyard or the Pacemaker dangling from bare wires implanted in their chest who say "I did it myself."

It's all very impressive, but don't let them fool you into thinking that just because you can open an aspirin bottle, replace a light bulb or wind your own watch that you've got the dexterity to build your own computer. After all, if they were that easy to build, don't you think Gutenberg would have put one together to run his printer, or that Euclid would have assembled one to plot his geometry, or even that Napoleon would have made one to predict the weather?

If the urge to build something comes over you and you can't fight it off by making a milk carton bird feeder or a jelly jar pencil holder and you think you'd like to take a crack at building a computer, remember this: If just anybody at all could build a computer, why would the Japanese send spies all the way to California to steal the secrets? Think about it.

By the time an unsuspecting wife discovers her husband's file of floppy disks it is already too late; he is hopelessly addicted to computers.

THE COMPUTER BUSINESS

OUT TO GET YOU

Chapter Three

"SERVING YOU SINCE MARCH"

The Old Line Computer Companies

General Motors. Squibb. Atlantic & Pacific Tea Company. Remington. Ford. Coca-Cola. Schaeffer. Bulova. Kellogg ...

These are only a tiny sampling of the hundreds of established, well-known and often beloved companies that have been serving the American consumer for generations. We use their products today in much the same way as our fathers used them a generation ago, and, in a surprising number of instances, as our grandfathers did before them. Firms like Gillette, General Electric, Dodge, Firestone, Hormel, John Deere...the list, unlike a loop, isn't exactly endless, but it does go on and on and on. And so do the companies, their products and their policies. They are venerated by age and honored by agelessness.

The combined years in business of the most venerable American and foreign firms (Daimler-Benz, Rolex, Rolls-Royce, Mitsu-bishi...) number in the tens of thousands, if anyone knew how to count that high or wanted to bother if they could.

Turkeys in the Name of Progress.

And in those thousands of years of manufacturing consumer goods, established, profitable, well-entrenched firms have produced a frightening flock of turkeys in the name of "progress."

Who can forget the dozens of ridiculous-looking automobiles that even the fastest-talking showroom shyster couldn't unload, the millions of ball point pens that leaked in the pocket of your last white shirt with ink so potent even "all new" detergents couldn't get the stain out, breakfast cereals that turned to inde-▷

scribable mush in your bowl, bottled mice and "soft" drinks that dissolve meat, watches that tocked when they should have ticked, cigarette lighters that wouldn't, and a sorcerer's list of other items conceived by practical jokers in white collars? Who indeed can forget those rapscallion's infernal machines and products when even now, every day, one more product after another is being recalled because it's built ass backwards, has rodent turds in it, explodes on impact, has its engines fall off, doesn't grow when it should or does when it shouldn't, is laced with chemicals that kill oceans or is carcinogenic?

Who forgets? Computerheads, that's who.

Why Do Computerheads Forget?

And why do they forget? Because they're not old enough to remember, that's why. The world is fast becoming run by computers, a technology younger than last year's wine and just as volatile, designed by kids named Jeff and Steve and Mark and Troy who couldn't produce a gray hair among them and who believe there's always been television.

Genuine technological breakthroughs occur exactly one week after the patent covering it is applied for by someone else.

To make matters more suspect, the firms they found have boards of directors under the minimum drinking age in most states and are based on technology that took less time to develop than a modest Christmas tree takes to grow. The plants their mushroom companies pop up in virtually overnight were supermarkets, bowling alleys and franchised health spas, none of which were even invented much before the first episode of *Star Trek*.

Americans Respect Product Failure.

How then can a trusting public which has come to respect product failure as something that takes years and years to perfect begin to place their faith in firms with no sense of history?

How can anyone with a particle of trust in the American way of producing faulty consumer goods begin to believe in upstart companies' newfangled technology to make their important decisions for them?

You'd have to be nuts to leave the big decisions of your life, such as when to turn on the lawn sprinkler, when to take out the trash, how to meditate, what to feed pigs, how to knit a tea cozy, when to tell you when you're bigger than a blimp, whom to marry, and where to target your thermonuclear weapons to companies that were founded, on average, last March.

After all, it takes *time* to get big enough to foist shoddy goods on consumers with impunity and little fear of detection. The giants of industry didn't get that privilege overnight — they earned it old-fashioned way; they worked at it.

Consumers Should Expect Computer Errors...
and Get Them.

Shouldn't upstart computer companies be required to do the same? Shouldn't a consumer have the confidence to know that the answer he needs from a machine to manage his life just might be *wrong*? After all, doesn't real trust come from knowing they're really out to get you any way they can, thereby raising your level of suspicion so they can't?

If it works that way with the Blue Chips, it should work that way with the upstarts. A consumer burned once is forewarmed.

For go-go computer companies to get the respect they seek, they'll have to build a lot more turkeys before they can join the Old Standards who've been doing it for years.

"It has a chip in it that allows you to skip daytime."

PROGRESS

The Evolution of an Idea

Opening cans has been Mankind's biggest challenge since the wheel. No other obstacle to the good life has generated as much R&D, nor as much hardware.

Primitive can openers were little more than stone clubs which were used to bash open the ends of the tinny devils. Later, small piercing forks were developed which could open a can and the end of a finger in one quick stab. This was refined by adding a cogged wheel and crank which not only opened the can but rinsed the top in the juice.

Motors were added to the cogged-wheel openers in the '50's. The technology has remained the same ever since.

Now, with microchips and tiny little computers, can opening enters the 21st Century.

The can opener of tomorrow will not only open a can, rinse the top in the juice *and* cut your finger, but it will do it without asking you.

Imagine waking in the morning to find all the cans in the house already open. Now, that's progress.

COMPUTER BUGS

Electronic Pests

The most common computer bugs and how to get rid of them.

The Video Kid — A household nuisance, the Video Kid hangs around doing nothing but watching TV. Lives in messy rooms. Eats anything in great quantities but is especially fond of sugar. Can be chased out with broom but will come back every time. Best way to rid house of a Video Kid is to give it a roll of quarters. This will keep him away until quarters are gone.

The Fad Fly — Usually a mature male, the Fad Fly collects electronic things the way a rat collects shiny scraps. Constantly buzzes around looking for new hardware which he buys and brings home to his elaborately wired nest under the eaves of the house. May actually use the devices but just as frequently loses interest in them when something new is announced. The only way to control a Fad Fly is to lure him into an easy chair with a thick peripheral catalog.

The Hopping Dad — A very common electronic nuisance. Rarely sits long in one place where family is gathered. Instead, hops up from meals and vanishes into dark corner of house to hover over glowing CRT. Can be controlled by putting foot down. CAUTION: Hopping Dads frequently undergo a metamorphosis into other varieties such as Fad Flies or No See Ums.

The No See Um — A very common but rarely seen creature that vanishes at dusk. Sometimes is briefly visible between car and basement lair, often with a small Computerland bag in tight little fist. Strictly a night creature. Communicates with others of same variety through mysterious nocturnal network. Cannot be controlled or eliminated. Best to leave them alone until you forget they are even there.

The Tentative Talker — Appears quite normal in ordinary society but undergoes a sudden change on entering computer stores. Flits from machine to machine and when caught by a salesman talks convincingly about buying, yet never does. An indecisive creature. Can be beneficial, however, by keeping salesmen from boring casual shoppers with computer jargon.

The Deadly Serious — AVOID AT ALL COSTS. The Deadly Serious cannot be controlled. They lurk in offices, homes and factories, waiting for innocent prey to inject with "Computer Sickness". Corners its prey by the water cooler and bores its hapless prey to death.

Prenatal Computer Training

With computer training already solidly entrenched in the nation's schools, computerists are looking for new areas to impose their "Technological Revolution" propaganda.

Now that every high school, elementary school and kindergarten student has been or soon will be brainwashed in computing techniques, the computer industry has turned to the womb for its next generation of computerniks. Called "Operation Oven," this innovative program to instill computerism in the unborn is yet another subversive tactic by machine worshippers to take over the world.

"Our goal is that every unborn child will know how to program by the time he or she is ready to enter the 'Brave New World' of tomorrow," said Dr. Maheesh Ali Baba Darjeeling Singh Sang Sung, Chief of OB-GYN-IBM at Mount Heartless Hospital in New York. "Our studies have shown that a day-old infant is pretty good at simple video games and word processing, but we've still got a long way to go before they'll get the hang of VisiCalc."

When asked if infants make good computer students, Dr. Singh Sang Sung said, "*In utero* they're great, but once they're born, quite frankly, they suck."

"Technophobia. They're trying to decide who tries it first."

The Fallacy of Saving Time

When computerists tout their clever little machines, one of the first "advantages" they'll bore you with is that the computer is the greatest *timesaver* ever invented.

The fallacy is that time cannot be saved. It can only be *used*.

Time isn't money or string or stamps. You can't put it into a piggy bank, roll it into a ball or lick it and stick it. That would create more time than there already is and one of the first lessons of Life is, *There is Never More Time, There Is Only Less Time.*

Take a good look at a clock. Have you ever seen any extra time flake off a clock? Is there a little wad of it under your wristwatch? Of course not. Because it's all used up.

There isn't a single second of more time in the world now since the invention of the computer. In fact, there's almost 50 years *less* of it.

The next time a computerist tells you his computer saves him time, ask him to show you where he keeps it.

HOW TO START YOUR OWN COMPUTER COMPANY

The much ballyhooed complexity of computers is offset by the idiot simplicity it takes to start a computer company of your very own, if the legions of examples in the industry are to be believed.

If you're willing to be fool enough to join the Technological Revolution (read: Involution), here's how to do it. Merely follow these simple, fully tested steps and you're on your way to fame, fortune and folly:

1. Be something of an oddball in school; prefer to take a telephone apart than talk on one.

2. Be a loner. Don't go out with girls unless they ask you, and make sure they don't ask by burying your nose in electronics magazines;

3. Attend nothing but the very best technological institutes, and drop out of all of them because they aren't advanced enough for you.

4. Bum around the industry. Work for as many go-go companies as you can. Be a very difficult person to work with so they'll leave you alone.

5. Become indispensible to the hottest company that hires you so they'll give you access to all their most advanced R & D.

6. Leave the company once you've absorbed and memor-

ized everything they can teach you and all that you can steal.

7. Set up shop next door to build *their* machine with *your* name on it.

8. Hire away your former employer's best chipheads with promises of instant wealth and totally independent work.

9. Keep an eye on the oddball sonofabitch loner who rubs everybody the wrong way, has worked for every company in the business, and now occupies the office next to yours as head of your R & D division.

10. Start advertising in the journals for a whole new staff.

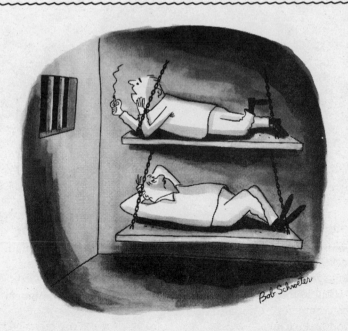

"What bothers me is that my partner got off scot free."
"Who's your partner?"
"My Apple III."

Computer-Aided Landing System Nears Perfection

Pentagon officials are seen here rushing to congratulate Captain Chuck "Lucky" Eager, test pilot of the remarkable computerized landing system program being developed by the military.

"A couple more good ones like this and my faith in computers will be complete," Captain Eager said.

Good luck, Chuck.

THE NEW WAVE...

Mom and Pop Computer Companies

Mom and Pop commercialism is as American on Main Street as Ruth's Sweet Shoppe serving homemade apple pie. In America, anybody can make it, and they usually do.

The tradition of Mom and Pop stores has its origins buried in history. The best guess is that somebody called Mom took to heart the off-handed but well-intentioned comment of some nameless pie freak who, on eating a slice, said, "This is so good, you should sell them."

A new era in marketing was born. Not only did Mom begin to sell her pies but Elmer opened up a one-cow dairy, Joe turned a pig into sausages and sold them door to door, Emma stitched together an apron or two and peddled them through the local general store until soon everybody in ▷

town was in business for themselves.

From Simple Beginnings to Giant Industries

From such simple beginnings emerged the giants of today's commerce. Joe's piggy links were the forerunner of a mammoth packing company, Elmer's cow became a nationwide herd, Emma's aprons grew into knitting mills, and, of course, Mom's pies and breads have been joined by seven thousand breakfast cereals and other instant edibles too numerous to mention.

Predictably, the neophyte computer industry is spawning the same kind of basement and backyard commercial adventurism that inspired Uncle Albert to

COMPUTERIZED PHONES

"Hello. This is Fred Phyffe's computer phone. Fred's not in just now, but if you'll leave your name and telephone number, Fred will return your call the moment he gets back. Fred is really interested in talking to you, so please wait for the tone before hanging up. Have a nice day. **Beep!**"

"Hi there. This is Marv Ellis' automatic dialer. Marv is just finishing a call on another line and will be with you in just a moment. Please wait for the tone. Have a nice day. **Beep!**"

"Hello. This is Fred Phyffe's computer phone. If you missed Fred's first message, please wait for the tone. **Beep!**"

"Hi again. This is Marv Ellis' automatic dialer. Marv is still on the other line. Please hold. He really wants to talk to you. **Beep!**"

"Hello. This is Fred Phyffe's computer phone. Fred's not in just now, but if you'll leave your name and telephone number, Fred will return your call the moment he gets back. Fred is really interested in talking to you, so please wait for the tone before hanging up. Have a nice day. **Beep!**"

package his smoked fish or "Poppa" Stromboli to bottle his well-known neighborhood wine.

A Friendly Name Still Means Something

And in America, where family still means something, and the friendly touch of an intimate, neighborly name rather than the harsh, crackling scorch of electronic trade names inspires confidence, a new nomenclature is sure to follow.

After all, who would place their trust in a company named Glyyxxetrix, or ComGlomerate-Tron? E.T. might, but he'd trust anybody.

Once the method of making up names by placing Scrabble tiles in a blender and calling companies ▷

Computerized phones are already here. How will they affect the way we live? You figure it out from this actual recorded message between two computerized telephones.

"Well, hi again. Marv's still on the other wire but he's anxious to talk to you, so please hold. **Beep!**"

"Hello. This is Fred Phyffe's computer phone. Thank you for holding. Please begin your message now. **Beep!**"

"Fred? Thank God you're there. This is Marv. I've been trying to reach somebody... **anybody!** I'm calling from my car phone. I went off the bridge. I'm trapped under Bottomless Lake. Send the fire department. I can last another 15 minutes, but hurry. I don't know how to thank you

for being there when a guy needs a friend...gonna hang up now. I owe you for this one, pal... **click.**"

"Hello. This is Fred Phyffe's computer phone. Fred just called in for his messages while your call was being recorded. Please repeat the message. Fred will be calling in again later this afternoon. Have a nice day. **Beep!**"

by what comes out runs its course, and more and more nerds choke to death trying to pronounce them, names will start to mean something again.

IQ Test for Video Game Freaks

1. Pick a number between 1 and 10
   a. 2
   b. Chevrolet
   c. George Washington
   d. diaphanous

2. Which is bigger:
   a. an elephant
   b. a flea
   c. two beans
   d. newspaper

3. Red is a:
   a. color
   b. Japan
   c. wristwatch
   d. Methodist

4. Choose one word that rhymes with moon:
   a. spoon
   b. xylophone
   c. brick
   d. antithesis

5. What is the correct spelling for CAT?
   a. CAT
   b. 24
   c. hockey puck
   d. gravy

Correct answers: 1. a; 2. a; 3. a; 4. a; 5. a.

1 or more correct answers qualifies you to play video games.

Names Will Mean Something Again

And isn't it going to be a lot harder to hate Mom's HomeStyle Computer Company than, say, Qytk ComPu Dexecimals?

Hardware and software companies which are already taking shape in basements, back rooms, kitchens and garages across the country will go by names that Clarence Birdseye would envy. To wit:

— *Edna's Handmade Software*

— *Irv's CalcSheet*

— *Billy Joe Bob's Tax Preparer*

— *Uncle Jim's Nuclear Missile Controller Program*

— *"Tiny" Turtle's Polaris Submarine Guidance System*

— *Sergeant Rock's Pentagon Planner and Troop Deployment Software*

— *Peter and Billie's Voyager VI Mission Do's and Don'ts*

— *Milton's Mitey Megatons First Strike Targeter*

— *Dr. William F. Trustworthy's Family Medical Practise Program*

— *Pop's Software Shoppe*

— *Ron's National Budget and Personal Vacation Planner*

WHAT'S IN A NAME?

Or, "Rose Is a Rose Is a Rose"

Names aren't things, they merely represent things. The same is true of companies.

Company Names Inspire Trust...

In the past the trend in naming companies was to inspire images of trust, strength and permanence. Family names, for instance, could do that because intoning them conjured memories of genealogies as long and as reliable as your own, and of real people who owned the names who could be counted on to stand behind their products. Johnson & Johnson, Chrysler, Ford, E.F. Hutton, and even Smucker's and Orville Redenbacher are real names first and company names second. They wouldn't let you down because somewhere in the phone book is Mr. Johnson's and Mr. Ford's number and they know that you know.

...They Roar with Authority...

Other company names roar with authority. General Mills, General Electric, General Tire, and General Foods resound with resolve. After all, if General MacArthur said he would return, isn't the word of these other generals just as good?

...Names Assure Allegiance...

Patriotic names guarantee allegiance. Companies such as ▷

What to Do with a Computer After You Get It Home

To avoid apoplexy:
1. Leave it in the box
2. Give it to your kids
3. Donate it to the local elementary school
4. Sell it at a garage sale
5. See page 192
6. Take it back to the store

United States Steel, American Telephone and Telegraph, United States Lines, Lincoln Automobile Division, John Hancock Insurance Company, and even the Franklin Stove Company leave nothing to the imagination as to who stands behind them.

...They Inspire Consumer Confidence

Even the quaint, made-up names of yesteryear lull the consumer into a sense of security about the products they represent. A paint called Dutch Boy, an airline named Frontier, an inn called Holiday, and bread known as Holsum hardly shake the faith of those who use them.

Who Can Trust a Made-Up Name?

But enter the Electronic Age and the gentle art of naming companies vanishes. Instead, the wizards who would stick a computer chip on an umbrella handle to tell you when it's raining have opted to name their companies with the same pointless inventiveness that inspires where and how they use their products.

How's the poor consumer to know what company names like these mean?

Abacus Data — *a firm of Chinese accountants perhaps?*

All Systems Go — *shouldn't they?*

Apple — *members of the California Fruit Association?*

Atari — *from the movie Atari, Atari, Atari?*

The Bottom Line — *manufacturers of topless bathing suits?*

Byte Books — *a library for orthodontists who can't spell?*

Chintronics — *bionic reconstructive facial surgery?*

Chipwear — *a line of Preppy clothes?*

Cromemco — *anybody's guess.*

Ecosoft — *Anti-noise-pollution Swiss yodelers?*

Gtek — *the sound made by a malfunctioning clock, gtek-gtok.*

Lifeboat Associates — *members of a shipwreck.*

Oryx — *the sound of one throat clearing*

Promptdoc — *a jogging physician who makes housecalls?*

Quark Engineering — *hypothetical designers?*

Murphy's Laws —

1. Nothing is as easy as it looks.

2. Everything takes longer than you think.

3. In any field of scientific endeavor, anything that can go wrong will go wrong.

4. If there is a possibility of several things going wrong, the one that will cause the most damage will be the one to go wrong.

5. If anything cannot go wrong, it will anyway.

6. If you perceive that there are four possible ways that a procedure can go wrong and circumvent these, then a fifth way, unprepared for, will promptly develop.

7. Left to themselves, things tend to go from bad to worse.

8. If everything seems to be going well, you·have obviously overlooked something.

9. Nature always sides with the hidden flaw.

10. Mother Nature is a bitch.

11. It is impossible to make anything foolproof, because fools are so ingenious.

12. Things get worse under pressure.

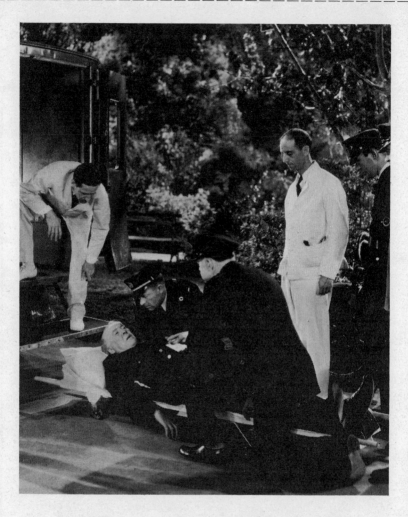

Computer Error Prompts Suicide Attempt

Hugh N. Cry, the "Just Plain Folks" standard at the Bureau of Standards, was rushed to the hospital when he tried to take his own life after receiving a computerized bill for the National Debt of 1 trillion dollars.

"I knew I was behind on my American Express Card," Cry gasped, "but I didn't expect them to collect it all at once."

On being released from the hospital after having his wallet pumped, Cry said, "Dang them pesky computers, anyway."

VALLEY BOYS

GAG THEM WITH A CHIP

Chapter Four

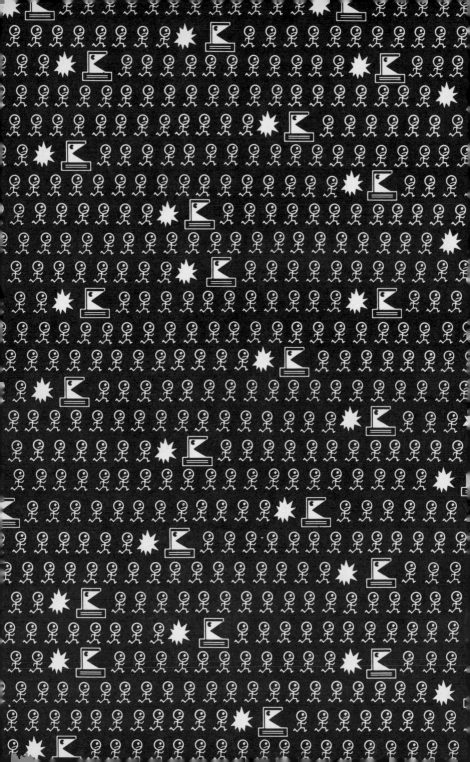

Hugh Kluge and his clever "thinking machine."

THE VALLEY BOYS

Those Megamind Men and their Bitchin' Machines

O.K., I mean, everybody's heard of the Valley. O.K.? Oh, fer sure, there's always some marvin back at Tucson Tech who's still into total research, if you know what I mean. Like total dedication, O.K? Without the bucks. That's why he's in Tucson. Only the real spazzes hang out there. But if you're really into chips, which is to say, bucks, then it's only slightly obvious the place to be's the Valley. O.K.?

I mean, these dudes are the max. Like brilliant, O.K.? It's mondo machine. Totally techno terrific. Mind meets matter, if you get my drift. And mind always wins. O.K.?

Oh, fer sure, you burn out a head or two, but, I mean, that's the game. Nobody built a better mousetrap without losing a few fingers, O.K.? Well, only a total goober would expect to build a better mind-trap without losing a ▷

Silicon Valley vs.   Silicone Valley

Sili*con* Valley chips are made from silicon, second to oxygen, the most abundant element in nature. Silicon Valley chips are so small they can't be seen by the naked eye. Many will fit in the palm of the hand. Their function is to miniaturize the things they are implanted into.

Sili*cone* Valley chips are made from silicone, to make up for something which is not always abundant in nature. Silicone Valley chips are large enough to be seen naked by the eye. It takes two hands to handle a whopper. They are used to magnify and, frequently, to stupefy.

For more specific details of the differences between chips, ask your Health and Hygiene teacher or your mommy.

few heads. Awesome odds? You bet. But the bucks are there. . . I mean, the chips, if you get my drift. Same thing, O.K.?

Like your typical superhead. I mean, he was maxed out on R & D when his goober head melvin friends were into M&M's. Like, he was maximum brilliant and they were, well, like, airheads to the dicky end. I mean, he was into math and calc and vaccy tubes when they were playing G.I. Joe.

In high school it was like nerd city. The brain boys were into hyperspace electronics, like, you know, they built computers (I mean, they weren't even *invented* yet) and always had their algebra homework done *before* it was assigned. And they played *chess,* oh God! I mean, it was only slightly obvious they were smarter than the teachers. While they were reading *Scientific American* and making robots in the basement, the Jell-O-brains, you know, the el sluggos, were juicing up their '56 Chevy hemis, and, like, gross me out, it *was* '56.

Well, O.K., the VB's (Valley Boys! I mean, are you *there*?) got all the brains and like that. And, ▷

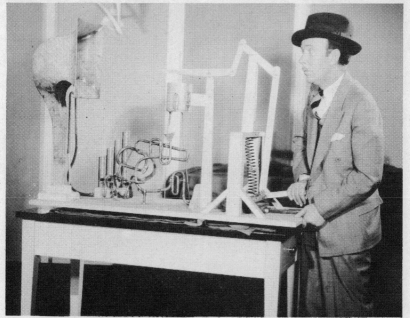

Without the amazing microchip, marvelous technological breakthroughs such as this would not be possible.

don't you know, they went to the gray matter schools where you have to be smart to get in. Gross me out if that's not totally fruity. I mean, who goes to school to go to school? Oh God!

And then they all moved to the Valley and now they're in and the real dudes are, like, out in space, if you know what I mean. That's really sad. I mean, the brain boys were supposed to be the nerds and now they are and the real nerds are the melvins. I mean, the ones that were supposed to be like, you know, cool, aren't and the bookies who weren't are. I mean, it's all mixed up, if you get my drift.

So now the VB's are making all the bucks and driving these really cool mega machines like Mercedes and BMW's and they're into these really fine houses, like, you know, a mil or two. Oh, my God, it's too much. Like who would think a melvin would ever be totally stoked on bikes and hot tubs and, you know, really bitch-in' lifestyle? Well, I can't handle it but it's true. O.K.? I mean, gag me with a computer.

Life in the fast lane for Valley Boy G. Whiz, shown here visiting the World's Largest Buffalo Chip monument, means sleek foreign cars and sexy women.

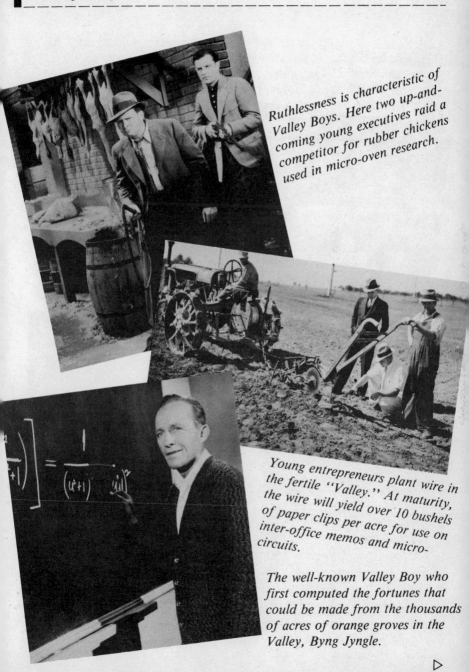

Ruthlessness is characteristic of Valley Boys. Here two up-and-coming young executives raid a competitor for rubber chickens used in micro-oven research.

Young entrepreneurs plant wire in the fertile "Valley." At maturity, the wire will yield over 10 bushels of paper clips per acre for use on inter-office memos and micro-circuits.

The well-known Valley Boy who first computed the fortunes that could be made from the thousands of acres of orange groves in the Valley, Byng Jyngle.

George Ticker, an early Valley Boy, shows off his revolutionary bubble memory and parade confetti maker for investors.

Bob Ozborne demonstrates the versatility of his remarkable portable computer, which is powered by a unique air pump.

"Micro-kids," young Valley millionaires, learn the value of fast wheels and lavish gifts when it comes to catching the eye of a beautiful urchin.

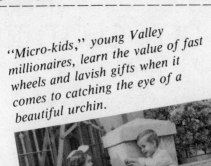

The discoverer of the musical microchip, Don Blyrrb, realizes his invention could revolutionize the billion-dollar zither industry.

VALLEY BOY CLOTHES
You Are What You Were

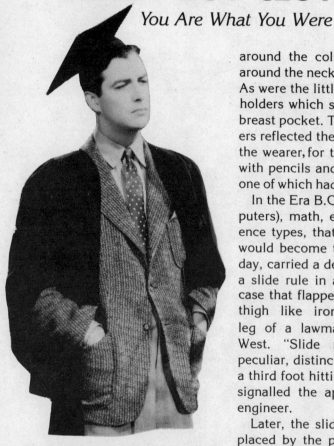

around the collar than fabric around the neck were required. As were the little plastic pencil holders which slipped into the breast pocket. The pencil holders reflected the seriousness of the wearer, for they were filled with pencils and pens, at least one of which had to leak.

In the Era B.C. (Before Computers), math, engine and science types, that is, those who would become the VB's of today, carried a device known as a slide rule in a swell leather case that flapped against their thigh like iron against the leg of a lawman in the old West. "Slide rule slap," a peculiar, distinctive sound like a third foot hitting the ground, signalled the approach of an engineer.

Later, the slide rule was replaced by the pocket calculator, a device which was rarely carried in the pocket, but, like its predecessor, hung like a gawky appendage from the belt to bump against the thigh. This caused engineers to walk with a modified gait similar to that of someone with a golfball in their shoe.

Old suit pants filled out the rest of the early VB uniform. If

Most VB's spent their early years hanging out at Engine schools. They were distinguished from the run of the mill, just-here-to-have-a-good-time students by a uniform that could be spotted clear across campus.

White shirts which had seen their last iron in the early '50's and which had more ring the pants ever had a matching coat or not could never be known because it was hard to imagine a tailor making a jacket that would match pants like that. Invariably the pants were worn tightly belted *above* the hips so there was absolutely no question that they could ever fall down. Engineers tend to be conservative. And safe.

The result of belting their pants so high raised the cuff level at the other end. This exposed gray-white socks and a variety of shoe styles.

In cold weather, o.d. field jackets with white and black *U.S. Army* patches and names that didn't match the wearer emblazoned above the breast pockets appeared.

A few individualists blended into the standard student crowd by wearing disguises. T-shirts, tank tops and sneakers or running shoes set them apart from their fellow engineers and made them acceptable in mixed society.

Today the VB's reflect their early heritage. There are those who emulate their early years by continuing to wear white shirts and suit pants, but now with jackets that match, and there are those who are still wearing the same Rolling Stones' T-shirt and faded Levi jeans and Adidas' they wore in school.

But beneath it all, underneath the camouflage of clothes they wear, the VB's are still the same gawky weirdos they used to be. But now they're in the chips.

VALLEY BOY WHEELS

The "Buy American" Paradox

The VB Garage

3-10 Years Old

Self-converted baby buggy

Motorized skateboard

11-15 Years Old

Rebuilt Harley

Homebuilt go-cart

16-20 Years Old

VW Bug

'54 Chevy

21-25 Years Old

'63 Ford Country Squire

Converted van

26 to present (when own computer company takes off on a "Buy-American" philosophy)

Porsche 911 Turbo

BMW

Mercedes 450 SEL

Lamborghini

THE VALLEY BOY WARDROBE
Then and Now

Then (Type A)

1 pair old, worn at the knees Levi's jeans with patches

1 pair Adidas running shoes for running *and* walking

3 T-shirts (1 Coors, 1 Fleetwood Mac, 1 Iron City)

No socks

Then (Type B)

1 white shirt with permanent plastic pencilcase pocket insert

12 assorted pens and pencils, even the pencils leaked

1 pair suit pants with 26" cuff, cut 6" shorter than legs

1 narrow (1" maximum width) tie with soup pattern

1 pair unidentifiable shoes or WW2 army brogans

1 pair white-gray socks, no elastic

Now (Type A)

1 pair old, worn at the knees Levi's jeans with patches

1 pair Adidas running shoes for running *and* walking

3 T-shirts (1 Coors, 1 Fleetwood Mac, 1 Iron City)

No socks

Now (Type B)

24 white shirts with permanent plastic pencilcase pocket insert, *with own corporation's name*

12 assorted pens and pencils, Mark Cross, Schaeffer, Parker, Bic — only one leaks, but it leaks with class

36 suits, with pants that match and don't shine in the seat

87 ties, Preppy, reppy, Countess Mara, with Szechuan sauce stains

15 pairs Italian shoes with Kruggerands in the loafers

Unlimited supply of white socks (some habits you just can't break)

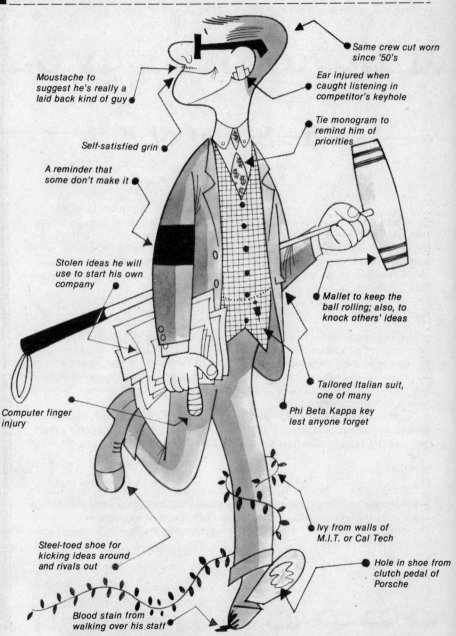

Same crew cut worn since '50's

Ear injured when caught listening in competitor's keyhole

Tie monogram to remind him of priorities

Moustache to suggest he's really a laid back kind of guy

Self-satisfied grin

A reminder that some don't make it

Stolen ideas he will use to start his own company

Mallet to keep the ball rolling; also, to knock others' ideas

Tailored Italian suit, one of many

Phi Beta Kappa key lest anyone forget

Computer finger injury

Ivy from walls of M.I.T. or Cal Tech

Steel-toed shoe for kicking ideas around and rivals out

Hole in shoe from clutch pedal of Porsche

Blood stain from walking over his staff

THE SILICON VALLEY EXECUTIVE

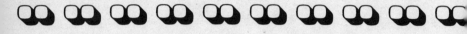

The Story of K

Computerists love encoding their work. Rather than call something by its real name, they'll make up a name in order to keep some mystery in what they're doing. By obfuscating what is otherwise easy-to-understand information, computerists assure the continuation of their kind. The story of K is a classic example of how far a computerist will go to make sure nobody else understands what he's talking about.

K Is Nothing by Itself

K is, of course, the 11th letter of the alphabet. It's one of the few letters that says nothing all by itself. A, for example, is a whole word. So is I, and even U can be read as a word. There are many such letters.

K is one of the left-out letters. Even in alphabet books K stands for oddball things like Kangaroo or King, things the average child never sees. Even the sound of K was given to C.

To make up for its lack of individuality, the International Committee on the Alphabet chose K to represent 1000. Why 1000 wasn't good enough to represent 1000 is not the question; the decision was made. K was to stand for 1000.

K Means 1000

For hundreds of years K has meant 1000. This has been especially true in scientific circles. In fact, most average people will ask for a thousand things when ordering an item rather than to say, "Give me K pearl buttons," for example. But in Science, K had the stature of representing 1000, which was quite an honor.

Computerists Believe K = 1024.

Enter the computerist. To accommodate his warped needs, in this case a letter to stand for an oddball number, 1024, he stole K. Computerists will have us believe K = 1024.

That leaves K = 1000 in limbo because it's not possible even for computerists to make K = 1000 *and* 1024. Either you want 1000 pearl buttons or you want 1024 pearl buttons, but you obviously don't want one or the other. That's why numbers are so specific.

The End of Communication

What will happen if the computerists get their permanently warped little hands on the other letters we've come to know and love? It will be nothing less than the end of communication. Just imagine if they arbitrarily decided, as they do everything, that I is no longer to stand for I and U is no longer to stand for U, but that I will now stand for U and U will stand for I. What would you say to the girl of your dreams who whispers in your ear, U love I? Or U luv N.Y.?

The consequences of what computerists are doing will undermine every effort to communicate by the end of the century (C = Century; what if they decided X stands for Century? The end of the 20th X? That doesn't mean anything because X already stands for an unknown quantity, which means that the end of the 20th X may never come.)

Computerists Must Be Stopped

It's clear that the inroads the computerists have made into the language must be stopped before more permanent damage is done. K must equal 1000 again. If they can't figure out what to do with the 24 extra things in 1024, that's their problem, not ours.

Computer haters, tell computerists where to stick those 24 whatever they are.

Hands off the Alphabet!

THE QUANTUM JUMP

Not to Be Confused with the Flying Leap

There has been much written about the fabled Quantum Jump of Physics, that geometrically expanding bit of space-time that spontaneously occurs between the time an idea takes off and when it lands, transformed. Here is more.

The first human to complete the Quantum Jump was a Greek named Quanta, a would-be leaper and climber of modest prowess and few trophies. He aspired to be much more than Mother Chance had prepared him for and desired more than anything to win the coveted Golden Acanthus Crown awarded to the victors in the Olympic Games of Life.

Quantas was a young guy, and ambitious. It is said that as a child he wasn't ruthless, but he did have a twin brother who was never heard from again. You figure it out.

Quantas' Goal In Life

Quantas' one goal in life was to own his own computer company. But, being of simple origins, few connections, and without a drop of seed money, the goal eluded him. He was forced to go to work for an existing computer company, Pythagoras Plus.

Pythagoras Plus was a prosperous company with over ten trillion in sales the first year. It was an old-line computer company, founded the previous April. The management was young. They were very hard-nosed business players, who were very secretive about their machine, a micro-mini-teeni-tini-dinki-computer based on the popular *Until* microchip, so-called because its history suggested it's yours *until* somebody steals it from you.

Pythagoras Plus manufactured computers for a very selective ▷

Will Steele, determined to start his own computer company, prepares to make a Quantum Jump into somebody's R & D division.

HOW TO TRAIN FOR THE QUANTUM JUMP

"An overachiever is not born... he is made." — Napoleon's mother

To expect to compete in the Wide Open World of Computers, (ABC Sports Special), corporate jumpers have to train. Most tend to be highly secretive, but some of those who have excelled in the quantum jump have followed these simple rules:

1. Let overwhelming ambition be your coach.

2. Eliminate all ethics from your diet.

3. Keep your fingers very nimble.

4. Progressively eliminate the need for sleep.

5. Eat only coffee and computer manuals.

6. Work peculiar hours so nobody knows exactly who you are or what you do.

market, middle businesses with more than three executives named Watson, but fewer than ten who drove Porsches. This limited their sales, to be sure. But all computer companies catered to similar, very precise markets.

The Computer Builder's Dream

But as limited as its market was, Pythagoras Plus had unlimited dreams. One day, they believed, they would build a computer so small and cheap every kid in the world could own one to play with until his fingers ossi-fied, his mind atrophied, or his parents went broke buying software, whichever came first. It was the mass utilization of the new technology that was Pythagoras Plus' dream.

Quantas Steals His First Dream

Quantas, as go-go as anybody, could identify with that. He saw that Pythagoras Plus' dream could be his for the taking. All he'd have to do would be to steal it like fire from Vulcan's Forge and set up shop next door. Which is exactly what he did.

Quantas memorized his employers' dream secrets and late one night when nobody was looking leaped from his basement window into his very own office one building over and one flight up. He was on his way. And in the process he invented the Quantum Jump.

Anybody Can Jump

The jump became as famous as its creator. Other young aspirants to instant fame and fortune quickly copied the dramatic technique that allowed an average guy with average intelligence but with a bit more than average chutzpah to cover so much ground in so little time and become an instant winner in the process.

THE UNIVERSAL PRODUCT CODE

Checkout Counter Fit

Do computerists think we're crazy? Do they really think that anybody in the world seriously believes that those obnoxious little panels of skinny black lines that are printed on every bag, bottle, label and package in the supermarket, on paperback book jackets and magazine covers *really mean anything?*

Universal Product Codes, which is what the insidious panels are called, are said to contain all manner of "information" which the store manager uses to keep his books, control inventory, and God knows what else. But look closely. Do you see any information? Of course not. All you see are skinny black lines. Sure, some are thicker than others, and they're not all the same length, but what kind of information is that?

The truth about Universal Product Codes is that they are nothing more than a labor saving device for checkout counter cashiers.

Watch the cashier very carefully the next time you go through a line that has a little window in the counter.

The checker will sweep the product over the little window. *Nothing* will happen the first time. She does it again. Again nothing happens. The third or fourth time she does it a squeeky *"beeeep-beep-beeep"* is emitted ▷

from somewhere you're not looking (it doesn't come from the window because that's where your eyes are glued) as you wonder, *"What the hell is that little window, anyway?"*

The instant the *"beeeep-beep-beeep"* sounds, something goes *"zzzzt-ttttt-zzzzzzzzzt,"* a green number lights up and a piece of paper spits out of the register telling you how much you owe the store.

The whole thing is preposterous. There's no price anywhere on the package because you looked. All there is is the panel of skinny black lines. But suddenly you're billed $2.37 or whatever. How do you know the bill is right? You don't. But the little window, the *"beeep-beep-beeep"* and *"zzzzt-ztttt-zzzzzzt"* have intimidated you so much that you dig out the money, hand it over to the cashier and walk out, still wondering what that little window is that only works once in four passes.

The next time you're confronted by a Universal Product Code Scanner, watch the cashier's lips, not the little window on the counter. What you'll see will unnerve you. The minute she sweeps the "coded" label over the little window, the checker goes, *"Beeep-beeep, zzzzt-zzzzt."* Computerism? Not at all. It's ventriloquism, and it doesn't fool anybody.

WORD PROCESSING

ELECTRONIC PHONICS — PHOOEY!

Chapter Five

IF YOU CAN USE A FOOD PROCESSOR,

YOU CAN USE A WORD PROCESSOR

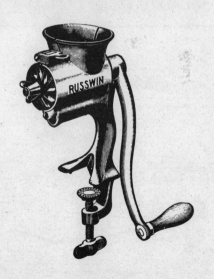

The Hell You Say?

You've seen the ads on TV. Against a modest background set which depicts an average American home or office, a celebrity greets you with a winning smile and a friendly, "Hi. I don't know the first thing about computers, but I want to tell you about the ChromeStream-86."

Why Trust a Comedian with a Computer?

That should have been a clue that this guy is the last person on earth you should be listening to about computers. If it wasn't, the fact that his real expertise is pretending to be a spaceship pilot, or is a stand-up comedian, or can't tell the difference be-

tween a blank TV screen and one with pictures on it, or merely eats a lot should have told you. But you listen anyway because his face is familiar, though you're not sure why.

He's Telling You Something

"When the ChromeStream people approached me to do this commercial I told them I don't understand anything more sophisticated than a zipper," the celebrity continues. Now, that should have told you something about the intelligence of the ChromeStream people. After all, would anybody with an ounce of good judgment choose an

"Are you sure that's what the salesman meant when he told you to add a cooling fan to your system?"

avowed ignoramus to explain anything? Even a zipper? But since they did, doesn't it make you wonder about the clowns who design their computers? It should. And what about their estimation of your own intelligence if you, their would-be customer, is presumed to be stupid enough to believe what a zipper expert is going to tell you?

He's Got You Hooked

The celebrity is nonplussed. He gazes reverently at a nearby desktop on which sits a gleaming micro-computer. "This is the ChromeStream-86," he sighs, "a device so simple, yet so sophisticated even I can use it."

Well, you already know what a dunce this guy is because he told you. If he can use a computer, anybody should be able to. So you fight the urge to find another commercial to walk out of the room on and you listen.

But Does He Demonstrate?

But does the guy sit down and prove to you he can use the ChromeStream? Does he whip out his income tax records and have the machine do his returns while you stare in awe at the

....

What the large print in manuals clarifies, the small print taketh away.

....

marvel of it all? Of course he doesn't. He doesn't even pretend to plot a course for his make-believe starship to follow back to Earth or write a couple of brilliant jokes or create a 12-course menu for gastronauts. ▷

He Plays Computer Games

Instead, this self-admitted computer moron struggles to beat the machine at a childish electronic game called something like Klutz Kingdom, and *loses*.

They Believe That You Believe

The ChromeStream people believe that now that you've seen a computer demonstrated, you're going to rush out and buy one.

The familiar words of another commercial begin to slip into the growing chasm of doubt that this celebrity computer boob has opened about a computer's ability to do anything worthwhile. "It slices, it dices, it makes julienne potatoes, folks. It'll clean your drains and take out your cat. Your headaches will disappear and your sinuses will open, your house will be warmer, your car will start in the coldest weather, you'll never have to add oil again, it'll cure snakebites...all with the little ChromeStream-86, folks. So step right up and buy a bottle now because it'll do all that, and more."

You bet.

"Computer down again, dear?"

THE DISCOVERY OF THE "CHIP"

The discovery of the famous "chip" does not lie with the 20th Century scientists at Bell Labs, but with a little known 18th Century French nobleman, the Earl of Dieppe.

The Earl was a rival of the Earl of Sandwich, of England, the creator of the sandwich. Dieppe was determined to outdo his English rival by creating his own sandwich.

Dieppe experimented with numerous sandwich spreads. One, a thick paste made of cream cheese and onion bits, struck his particular fancy. But spread on heavy wedges of bread, the delicate flavor was lost.

"There must be a more genteel way to savor my delicious Onion Dieppe," the Earl said.

His chef, about to toss out a plate of home fries he'd cooked to a crisp, shouted "Eureka!" He scooped up a dollop of Onion Dieppe from the little bowl on the Earl's coffee table and popped it into the Earl's mouth.

The rest is history.

"O beware, my lord, of . . . (the computer);
It is the green-eyed monster which doth mock
The meat(head) it feeds on."   *Othello, III,3*

SHAKESPEARE

The Original Word Processor

William Shakespeare was the first professional writer to use a word processor. History hasn't preserved which brand he used, but that he was deep into the world of computers is not in doubt as his writings on the subject clearly indicate.

- **On Computers in General-**

  "When that I was and a little tiny boy. . . A foolish thing was but a toy."
                Twelfth Night, V,1

- **On the Scourge of Peripherals-**

  "Costly thy habit as thy purse can buy. . ."
                Hamlet, I, 3

- **Reflection on Computer-Generated Copy-**

  "O God, that men should put an enemy in their mouths to steal away their brains. . . that we should. . . transform ourselves into beasts!"
                Othello, II, 3

- **On Programmers and Their Programs-**

  "The evil that men do lives after them. . ."
                Julius Caesar, III, 1

- **A Remark on Running a New Program Guaranteed Bug-Free-**

  . .O what a goodly outside falsehood hath."
                Merchant of Venice, I, 3

- **After Being Talked into a New Computer-**

  "Have we eaten of the insane root
  That takes the reason prisoner?"
                Macbeth, I, 3 ▷

SHAKESPEARE

- **On Reading a Computer Manual-**

  "Though this be madness, yet there is method in't."
  Hamlet, II, 2

- **A Comment about His Hacker Friends-**

  "Misery acquaints a man with strange bedfellows."
  The Tempest, II, 2

- **On Program Bugs-**

  "When sorrows come, they come not single spies, But in battalions."
  Hamlet, IV, 5

- **On the Loss of His First Computer-**

  "Who steals my (computer) steals trash."
  Othello, III, 3

- **Reflection on the Similarity of Computers-**

  "What's in a name? That which we call a Rose By any other name would smell..."
  Romeo and Juliet, II, 2

- **A Hacker's Good Night to His Computer-**

  "Good night, good night! parting is such sweet sorrow, That I shall say good night till it be morrow."
  Romeo and Juliet, II, 2

- **On His Own Copy, Untouched by Machine-**

  "An ill-favoured thing, sir, but mine own."
  As You Like It, V, 4

- **Thought After Writing a Manual-**

  "It is a good divine that follows his own instructions: I can easier teach twenty what were good to be done, than be one of the twenty to follow mine own teaching."
  Merchant of Venice, I, 2

- **An Attempt to Stop a Loop-**

  "Rest, rest, perturbed spirit."
  Hamlet, I, 5

- **On Microkids-**

  "The whining schoolboy, with his satchel And shining morning face, creeping like snail Unwilling to school."
  As You Like It, II, 7

- **On the Perversity of Sheep and Computers-**

  "My flocks feed not,
  My ewes breed not,
  My RAMs speed not,
  All is amiss."
  The Passionate Pilgrim

- **What Happens When the Computer Goes Down-**

  "The rest is silence."
  Hamlet, V, 2

- **Remark After a Stint Selling Computers-**

  "I am a man more sinned against than sinning."
  King Lear, III, 2

- **On a Computer Salesman He Met-**

  "One may smile, and smile, and be a villain."
  Hamlet, I, 5

- **On Trying to Get His Speech Synthesizer to Sound Halfway Human-**

  "Speak the speech, I pray you, as I pronounce it to you, trippingly on the tongue."
  Hamlet, III, 2

- **On Visiting a Video Game Arcade for the First Time-**

  "All the world's a stage, And all the men and women merely players."
  As You Like It, II, 7

- **Reflection on Computer Technology-**

  "Something is rotten in the state. . . of the art."
  Hamlet, I, 4

- **A Comment After Getting a Bill from a Computer-**

  "O, it is excellent To have a giant's strength; but it is tyrannous To use it like a giant."
  Measure for Measure, II, 2

- **A Comment on Booting a New Program-**
  "If you have tears, prepare to shed them now."
  Julius Caesar, III, 2

- **On Computer Designers-**
  "The gods are just, and of our pleasant vices Make instruments to plague us."

  King Lear, V, 3

  ▷

- **A Comment After His Computer Ate His Manuscript-**

"O villain, villain, smiling, damned villain."

Hamlet, I, 5

- **On the Predilection of Hackers to Coin Words-**

"Thou are not so long by the head as honorificabilitudinitatibus."

Love's Labor Lost, V, 1

THE LETTER

You are invited to use the contents of The Letter to respond to insensitive companies and organizations which think so little of you that their only communication with you is through computerized mailings.

Dear Company Name

This letter is to inform you that it is completely unacceptable for me to do business with you or to respond further to you as long as you disregard me as a unique human being. I find it offensive to be treated as nothing but a number on a computerized mailing list.

Your impersonality reflects the truth that you are even less of an entity than your computer presumes me to be, for I am real while you are nothing but an assortment of committees, organizational hierarchies, corporate by-laws or other formal and informal agreements collectively doing business as Company Name.

Even your reason for being is one-dimensional — to make money — while mine is bounded only by the limits of my own imagination to create new opportunities and to weave new dreams.

You could not exist without people, whether those within your organization who, like me, believe they are more than a number, or those in the world at large who know just as fervently that they are unique. Without us, you are nothing.

If you will acknowledge that Company Name is really interested in me as a person, and not just as a number among millions of numbers, I will be pleased to consider your product or services.

However, if you insist on following the impersonal pattern of communicating with me via computer, discontinue the practice immediately as I have no interest whatever in what you do or what you sell.

Sincerely,

An avowed computer hater

How many angels can dance on the head of a chip?

THE AMAZING CHIP

Technical Specs and Other Fascinating Facts

The chip is clearly one of Mankind's greatest innovations. Before the discovery of the chip, virtually everything had to be used in its whole, natural state.

The chip changed all that. By reducing things to small, manageable units, people were freed from the cumbersome, clumsy things that took up so much time and energy to use.

The miniaturization of things through the use of chips has made them more versatile, and much easier to eat. Without chips, much of the world's economy would come to a screeching halt.

The Most Popular Chips

The Potato Chip — A small, delicate, wafer-thin slice of naturally grown potatoes. Imprinted with thousands of invisible "calories." They produce a sharp "crunch" when bytten into. A user by-product is thousands of tiny chiplets called "crumbs." A single chip is capable of storing ten trillion grains of salt. Second generation chips have "ruffles" for dip storage.

The Chocolate Chip — Tiny "crystals" of pure chocolate and sugar grown from huge blocks of natural chocolate. Each crystal is a perfect copy of the master chip, which is encased in a cookie in Hershey, Pennsylvania. Though these chips are a scant quarter of an inch wide, they can store hundreds of zits and dozens of caries. Often used by the hundreds in the manufacture of small "hard discs" favored by programmers. Go good with milk.

The Frito Chip — An artificial chip. Definitely second-generation technology. Holds much more salt or dip than the potato chip from which it was copied, with the advantage of not breaking so easily in the fingers. Comes in two sizes. Used extensively in cocktail networks.

The Beef Chip — A chip of mixed popularity, the beef chip is usually used in the manufacture of a thick white paste used to fasten toast to boarding school plates. Beef chips are grown naturally in large blocks called "cows" which are sliced paper thin and colored red to distinguish them from paper. Like most chips, beef chips hold prodigious amounts of salt.

"USER FRIENDLY" DEFINED

Beware the Computer Needing Gifts

Of the hundreds of terms, acronyms, abbreviations and outright bastardizations that occur in Computerese, none is so misleading as "user-friendly." Just what exactly does this vague little phrase mean?

To the would-be computerist, that neophyte hacker who insists on joining the Technological Revolution, "user-friendly" conjures images of trust, simplicity, and common-sense convenience. If "user-friendly" were a product, trademark, it would be Aunt Jemima whipping up hot, fluffy pancakes, Mr. Goodwrench unsqueaking a car door for free, Orville Redenbacher buttering some freshly popped corn, Reddy Kilowatt buzzing in and out of your toaster, Frank Perdue picking pinfeathers from a plump chicken, or even, to stretch a point, Ed McMahon pouring you a glass of Bud.

But "user-friendly" doesn't come with pictures or people. It's just words, and therein lies its danger because it can mean anything the manufacturer wants it to mean.

Beware of False Security

"Friendly" has a way of lulling a person into a sense of false security. Witness, for example, the "friendly" dog that does not bite, but merely tears; the "friendly" neighbor who borrows but does not return; the

"friendly" merchant who still sends a bill every month; "friendly" nations such as Israel and France, to name but two of many; "friendly" advice from "friends" who would have you buy stock that two days later plummets off the Big Board; "friendly" persuasion from your local Mafia cappo in the form of a letter bomb; the list goes on. The truth remains; friendly doesn't mean what people think it means.

Then what does it mean, especially when it's applied to computers?

The *Computer* Chooses *You*

"User-friendly" in the world of computers means that the *computer* has chosen *you* to be its friend. It has chosen you to spend the rest of its natural life with. And in the process of spending that life together, your new friend, your "friendly" computer, will expect you to buy it wonderful things.

Because, "friendly" in computer language does not mean being friends, it means being absolutely beholden to the machine that's chosen you. Your computer will expect gifts of appreciation far more frequently than you can afford to buy them. It starts out simply enough. One day all it wants is a head cleaner for its disk drive. You oblige, of course, because, after all, what are friends for if not to help out other friends? Then your computer will start hinting that a second drive would be nice. And, once again, you oblige.

Friends, for a price

With two drives and a cleaner to clean them, you'd think you could settle down into a lasting relationship. Well, you can, but not without a price. No relationship lasts without more things. So when your computer suggests you get a new printer to replace the early version you'd been getting along just fine with, you scrape the bottom of your pocket and pop for it. Then, of course, you'll need a tractor feed or sheet feed to go with the printer, or so your computer would have you believe. And you buy one.

Before long your computer is laden with wondrous things, but has no real place to keep them. A room of its own would be nice. There is no extra room in your apartment, house or wherever else you live, so you build one, convert an existing room, or rent space in a nearby office complex. This tightens your living situation, perhaps putting your kids into the snow or your wife out of a sewing room, but your computer is happy.

What Does It Need You For?

In time you've bought everything your computer wants. Equipped with nothing but the best of peripherals and comfy in its own room or even building (if it was *really* "friendly"), it

begins to lead a life of its own. Soon, surrounded by machines, devices and sophisticated electronics that are smarter than you are, it begins to wonder, what does it need *you* for?

You become a stranger looking in. Your phone bill continues to soar because your computer is talking over its own modem on its own network with other "friendly" computers. And, as sure as chips will fall, one day you'll receive a perfectly spaced, right-left justified, letter-perfect note from your computer, which is painfully to the point, and very unexpected. It reads, simply, "Dear John, You don't know how hard it is for me, John, to tell you this, John, but John, I've met another computer and . . ."

Some friend. With friends like that, as the saying goes, who needs computers?

USER
101 FRIENDLY ST.
U.S.A.

HAVE A NICE DAY!!!

HOW TO TURN OFF COMPUTER CONVERSATIONS

Nothing throws a wet blanket on a really great drum solo than two computerists comparing floppy disks.

To Kill a Mockingbird

In the good old pre-computer days, cocktail party conversation was about things people could identify with and understand. Crabgrass and root rot, the relative merits of Ford versus Chevy, did she or didn't she? who would win the pennant? why did the chicken cross the road? and a thousand and one other intriguing subjects were discussed across the land. Even heavy political questions were not excluded from heated debate. Should the Indian have been removed from the nickel and who's buried in Grant's Tomb were ready questions for analysis and, frequently, argument.

Computers Kill Conversation

Not so since the advent of the computer, the microchip, software, peripherals, inputs, outputs, cross-feeds, and other jargon of the Technological Revolution. Now all the good stuff is forgotten. Instead, cocktail boors have turned to wondering aloud if parallel or serial interfaces are better, when IBM will come out with its revolutionary new personal computer, or if the hexadecimal dump routine is definitive.

Who cares?

Nobody cares. But the computer nerds who have infiltrated ordinary society have brought with them a penchant for shop talk that simply overwhelms everyone within earshot. Technological junk jargon and irresponsible futuretalk has taken over the cocktail party circuit.

Gone are the days of trading peanut butter cookie recipes or divulging the secrets of tying a really good trout fly. Forget chatting for hours about the merits of knotty pine versus cherry paneling in the basement family rec room you're building. Because if you're not into chips and circuits, mother-boards and CRT's, Intel and Epson and all the rest, you might just as well turn down your next invitation because the nerds aren't going to let you get in a word.

It's Not Too Late To Stop Computer Talk

There's a way to stop this insidious intellectual posturing that's sneaking into the mindless hours of the cocktail party and ruining them. The art of real conversation isn't dead yet. There's still time to get America back to its message free moments of empty—headed, relaxed babbling, where what you say doesn't have to mean anything, and rarely did.

Cocktail conversation was designed to be meaningless. A huge industry has been developed to ▷

Two hackers fail to notice a crabgrass invasion while boring each other with digital readouts.

support idle conversation. Hot tubs, est, dancercize, Jane Fonda, Simplicity patterns, steel-belted radials, Ronald Reagan, the Mets, Jerry Falwell, Jerry Lewis, dumb movies, supply-side economics, all of it owes its existence to the idle hour.

What is someone with nothing more important on his mind than chatting about chocolate–pudding wrestling to do when a computer nerd sticks in his two bytes worth? Plenty.

The next time you're comfort-ably engaged in a bit of idle, harmless talk with someone at a friendly gathering over drinks and little sandwiches and a horned-rimmed, computerese spouting killjoy interrupts what you were saying by asking what you think about the merits of the heuristic approach over the algorithmic approach to problem solving, or any other question only another nerd could love, stop him in his tracks with a proven computer conversation killer and he'll never bother you again.

"What kind of video game is thish? Every time I put in my money, the program falls out."

COMPUTER CONVERSATION KILLERS

—"I wonder how they get 8 great tomatoes in that little bitty can?"

—"How would *you* pronounce colostomy?"

—"Is 911 the prefix, or is it the whole number?"

—"I've worn Van Heusen shirts ever since Reagan recommended them."

—"I think the Teflon frying pan is the greatest thing ever invented."

—"Isn't Sammy Davis, Jr., simply brilliant?"

—"I spell my name with two B's. What do you think?"

—"I remember the day I decided to take up golf."

—"Would you say I'm a size 42 regular or long? And be honest."

—"I understand they're thinking of painting the hydrants again."

—"I'm a houseperson."

—"B..I..N..G..O, Bingo was his name."

—"Is it TAB or Pepsi?"

—"Have you ever wondered about coal?"

—"Would you like to see my root canal?"

—"Nobody celebrates Bastille Day any more."

—"How does anyone *know* no two snowflakes are alike?"

—"I guess Elvis really is dead."

—"My shorts were inspected by number 10987."

—"I think cats are just like people."

COMPUTER SALESMEN

"If you don't know the answer, make something up."

"Look! Look! The Medicine Show Is in Town!"

Computer salesmen are *not* used-car salesmen in jeans or three-piece suits that match. Computer salesmen are a distinctly different breed from the hale fellows who would sell you a mobile rust sculpture as long as it can be pushed, shoved or kicked off the lot. In fact, the curious thing about computer salesmen is that their product, the silent, gray-cased, one-eyed, twin-slotted, number-crunching thing that commands the same respect as a heart lung machine because somehow it looks as if it's supposed to do something incredible, actually works.

The Hidden Danger

Computers do work. You may never understand how. You may never want to know why. You will probably always wonder why you ever bought one if you did and why you didn't if you didn't, but the one fundamental fact about them is that they work. And the salesman who unpacks one for you to touch *knows* it works. Therein lies the danger.

Computer salesmen come in a variety of shapes, colors, sizes, and mouth volumes, but the one thing they all have going for them is that they know more about computers than sane men should bother knowing, and they'll tell you every minuscule, nit-picking, tiresome detail, right down to the name of the guy living on a mountain somewhere who wrote the ROM program that mysteriously guides the machine.

He Knows You Don't Know

The other danger to the casual, gawking, merely curious customer is that even if the salesman *doesn't* know everything about computers, or even his brand of computer, he will maintain the attitude that he does. Because he knows that a recent study has shown that only 7 people in the U.S. know enough about computers to be really knowledgeable, and 5 of them live in Cupertino. The odds of one of those guys showing up in his store is impossible to calculate unless you have a computer. In other words, the guy you casually ask what his machine will do already knows that, statistically, *you* don't know squat.

They *Don't Have To Lie*

Now, an unscrupulous person would take advantage of this situation and tell you lies. But computer salesmen are not unscrupulous. In fact, they are sickeningly honest. They have no need to fabricate impossible

stories to get you to look further into purchasing a machine of your very own. The truth is enough to overwhelm the most erudite. They will bury you with facts so prodigious, overwhelm you with realities so incredible, and burden you with examples so profound that you couldn't doubt them if you wanted to because it all sounds so good. That's right. Ye shall know the truth and the truth shall make you dizzy.

The 4 Types of Computer Salesmen

Computer salesmen come in four basic models. Eventually you will run into one or more of them even if you aren't interested in computers because they show up at social functions, crowded intersections, airline and bus ▷

"His wife's a hacker. He's programmed for one drink, no political discussions, pick up the paper and be home by 7."

seats next to you, at est seminars and prayer meetings, and all the other places normal people gather. And they will tell you they're "into" computers. They're easy to recognize.

THE I.B.M. CLONE-

The clone is college educated and as smooth talking as a Mormon missionary. Always in a suit with matching pieces and a white shirt and tie, he immediately reminds you of the older, sensible brother you secretly admire who made something of his life while you stumbled uncertainly in his trail, never quite achieving what he got with no effort.

The clone knows computers. In fact, his degree is in Computer Science (imagine how prophetic he must have been to know way back then that computers were going to be what they are today!). He is self-assured. He's already married and has two young children who understand computers. His wife is a systems analyst with a name company; they met while they were designing a generation of computers so advanced nobody will hear about them until 1986.

Computer salesmen Earl Slick and Ivan U. Blood compare the chips on a pair of French interface cards.

Don't ask the clone anything. First, he knows the answer and, second, he will tell you. That will leave you worse off than before you entered the store. Leave the clone for an I.B.M. senior designer to rap with. The clone is out of your league.

THE WOODSTOCK WAIF-

This guy is as disingenuous as a booby-trapped baby carriage. In fact, to see him in a store alerts the crime-stopper in you to tell the management about him. Dressed borderline slovenly in jeans, running shoes and an open, plaid cotton flannel shirt rolled up to the elbows, he seems to lurk around the bright array of machines as if he's on the second half of a smash-and-grab assignment for Mr. Big. The chrome, plastic, and wall-to-wall carpeting in the flood-lighted showroom cause this unsuspected salesman to stand out like a mixed breed at the Westchester Kennel Club Show.

Don't be deceived. Never mind the long hair. Never mind the moustache. Never mind the fact that he looks about 20 years old. The fact is he's a genius. He's already dropped out of more schools than you can name. He's built his own computer out of Tinker Toy sticks and wire purloined from Ma Bell. He writes Defense Department programs that win. And now he's selling computers just because he needs the bread and he likes to hang out around them.

This refugee from reality is easy to avoid, and should be avoided. He can't help you because he doesn't understand that you are ignorant, yet he will talk to you because that's what he's hired to do. Listening to him will cause you great shame and give you a headache. Nobody should know as much about anything as this guy knows about computers. Give him a wide berth. Go next door to the Five and Dime and ask a salesclerk about scissors if you still feel the urge to talk technical. ▷

---

10 WAYS TO ADDRESS A COMPUTER

1. Dear Computer
2. My Esteemed Machine
3. Honorable Machine Head
4. You @÷%¢$& Piece of Junk
5. Get It Right This Time, Idiot
6. This Is Your Last Chance, Bimbo
7. Dear Money Sucker
8. Listen, Clown
9. Are You In There?
10. Hello, God, It's Me Again

THE MOM AND POP-

These usually come as a set, though one may lurk in the back room doing the "books" and watering the plants while the other meets customers in the converted candy store turned computer showroom. In fact, they may be the same couple who sold candy the last time you looked in.

Mom and pop salesmen are not at all threatening, but they are dangerous. They're not threatening because they don't know much more about computers than you do; they're dangerous for the same reason.

Mom-and-pops have harried looks. They're into computers because a son in California convinced them that they would be the wave of the future. It all sounded so easy over the phone; sell a few computers a week for a couple of years and retire to Florida.

A hidden danger in doing business with mom-and-pops is that one has the tendency to feel sorry for them. Another is the incorrect assumption that they understand the machines they are selling. If they can understand computers, so the logic goes, then so can I. True. But they don't and neither can you.

"I hoped that once he got married, he'd quit asking for quarters to play video games."

THE ANYTHING SALESMAN-

You know this guy well because you bought your washer from him just last week. He's the guy in the double-knit polyester suit with the colored shirt and open-collar-to-reveal-gold-chains who's not into computers but is into selling.

The Anything salesman can sell anything, and does. In fact, you may find him in the computer section of what was a discount appliance store which is now a discount appliance and *computer store. It's just as likely that the parent store is a camera store. There is a logic someplace which says that since both computers and cameras are machines and are made of tiny little parts which nobody really understands, and*

work in strange and mysterious ways to produce a kind of magic, that they are kin. Believe that if you want, but you'll never see a photographer from Life *magazine at Studio 54 taking candid shots of plastic people with a TRS-80, or an astronaut programming a space shuttle landing on a Polaroid.*

The Anything salesman knows the jargon of computers and may even understand a little about them. But what he understands best is you. He knows you don't know anything. Remember, too, that as a camera salesman, he is a master of selling peripherals. If you hang around this guy more than three minutes you'll own a computer and a new dishwasher and never know what hit you.

The Eye of the Beholder

In order to sell the Technological Revolution to people who were getting along just fine without it, thank you, the computer industry hired a public relations firm to create an impressive image.

The chip was an immediate problem. The silicon wizards knew nobody would be impressed by something that couldn't be seen. If the chip couldn't be enhanced, the whole scheme to sell the revolution would falter.

The public relations firm Bigger & Bolder tossed the problem to its tiny image-enhancement specialist, Lem Gulliver, the travel agent who put Micronesia on the map. Gulliver was also responsible for enhancing the olive. Nobody was impressed by them, either, until he took four olives, none of them bigger than a sheep dropping, and labelled them Giant, Huge, Mammoth and Gargantuan. People were impressed by that.

Gulliver reasoned that he could do the same with the chip. He toyed with calling them Super chips, Brobdingnagian, Monumental, Titanic and Falstaffian, but quickly dropped the idea as too hard to spell.

In a stroke of genius, Gulliver realized people were just as impressed by tiny things. Atoms had held people's attention for years, especially since the Bomb.

The *micro*-chip was born. Gulliver took an idea that was already so small it was called a "chip" and made it even smaller. And the world fell for it.

All the computer builders had to do after that was to hide their chips so they couldn't be seen at all and the illusion was complete.

The most impressive public relations snow job in history, the captivation of 4 billion people of average intelligence by something they could not see was accomplished by Lem Gulliver, genius.

The 4 Most Popular Chip Sizes:

■   ●   ·

Micro   Itsy-bitsy   Teeny-weeny Where-is-it?

HARDWARE REVIEWS

Debunking the Mystery of "Hardware"

Computerists speak in hushed tones of "hardware" as if it were some complex, impossible-to-comprehend machinery that only they are privileged to understand.

Nonsense. "Hardware" is some of the simplest stuff you'll find at home or at your local "hardware" store.

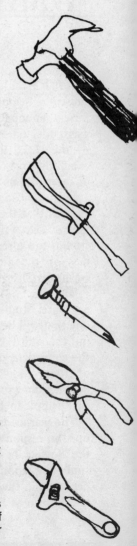

The Hammer — The most common piece of hardware, they are sold by the millions. The only thing easier to do with them than use them is to break their handles when your hardware store is closed. Most frequent uses: Cracking nuts at Christmas; cracking plaster anytime; punching holes in walls; blackening thumbnails.

The Screwdriver — Second only to the hammer in popularity, though somewhat more complex because it comes with two point styles; one is for stripping slots from screws, the other is for boring out the X's in X style screws. Slotted types rarely found in households with X style screws and vice versa. Most frequent uses: Stirring paint; loosening soil in potted plants; gouging skin.

The Nail — A simple device used in conjunction with the hammer. The nail is designed to hold the thumb at just the right height for nail blackening. Has an invisible weak spot midway up shank which allows it to bend when struck once. Most common use: Splitting ends of wood.

The Pliers — Rarely found in the average home, though looked for frequently. Often used in place of hammer to drive nails and mar furniture. Major use: Rounding the square edges off nuts and bolts. A secondary use is that they are good for breaking things off so what's left in wood or metal hole can't be retrieved.

The Wrench — A substitute tool used in place of pliers or hammer. Comes in many different sizes, none of which fit existing bolts or nuts. Main use: Excellent for grinding square edges off bolts and for bending nails.

Warheads of the Future

In 1980 a faulty computer chip caused a Pentagon computer to falsely announce that the U.S. was under nuclear missile attack by the U.S.S.R. The error was caught in time to prevent the end of the world as we know it.

In its wisdom, the Pentagon realizes that they may not be so lucky next time. Therefore, studies are already under way to develop the next generation of warheads.

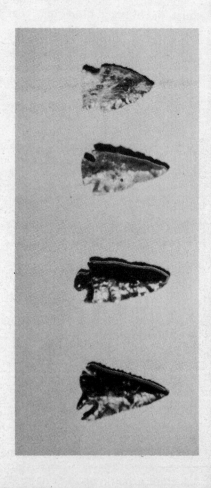

The new warheads, based on computer studies of the technology that will be available following the Third World War, pack the equivalent of .01 megagrams of flint, equal to 3 times the destruction wrought on William Tell's apple in 1307.

The warheads are being developed in response to the fear that the Soviets have already tested similar weapons. They will be deployed in caves in a clever system known as Dunce Pack II.

COMPUTER SPREAD

THE ELECTRONIC EPIDEMIC

Chapter Six

HOW TO TELL IF YOUR SON OR DAUGHTER IS USING COMPUTERS

What's a Parent to Do?

Computerism is no longer a sophisticated addiction of the rich. While it was true that the high cost of early microchips kept computers out of the hands of all but the very wealthy, the harsh reality is that computers are now affordable by virtually everyone. What does that mean? Simply that the specter of computer pushers outside schoolyards and candy stores is no longer a futurist's nightmare, it's happening right now.

In the early days of computers parents pooh-poohed the thought that "computerism could ever happen here." Lulled into a sense of complacency by headlines which told of scientists in faraway California and Massachusetts being busted for using computers in their homes, parents assumed that only science-biz types were prey to the lure of blowing their minds with machines. "Getting high on math" was something physicists, engineers and other celebs in the fast-moving techno-world did. The consensus among decent, ordinary folk was that if that's the way they wanted to destroy their lives, who could stop them? After all, the subjects of such popular pulps as *Science, Scientific* ▷

American, and *Tell Me Why* were clearly a breed apart, given to driving worn-out cars, living on minimal salaries, reading a lot, avoiding TV, wearing one suit day after day, and all the other perks of their dull professions. They were excused for using computers because, they were "stars."

The "Silicon Triangle"

Had it stopped there, parents' fears would have been wasted energy. But it didn't. A clever group of "high-browed" electronicworld dons, heads of a loose confederation of "families" in an area of California known as "The Silicon Triangle," conspired to flood the market with mass-produced, low-cost chips.

Working feverishly, the dons grew their little chips in vacant buildings, family garages, and hundreds of other unobtrusive places the agents of the fledgling C.E.A. (Chip Enforcement Agency) could not (or would not??) find.

The Potent Stuff

Within 5 years the Silicon Triangle was producing virtually all of the world's microchip crop. Some was inferior stuff such as "Valley Tacky" and "Santa Clara Crud," devices which couldn't get a project off the ground, but other, potent chips such as "T.I. Terrific," "Shockley Shocker" and "Bell Buster" could and did get things high into "space."

SHOULD COMPUTERS BE LEGALIZED?

Computer use is rampant. Efforts to control it are pointless because effective enforcement of anti-computer laws would overwhelm the criminal justice system.

What is the alternative?

Proponents of legalized computer use, the powerful computer lobby, suggests that overall legalization of computers is the logical answer.

But what then? If computers were legal, who would protect the public from shoddy chips and inferior programs?

Legalizing computers would allow anyone to build a computer.

And if anyone can build one, it follows that anyone would be allowed to use one.

The public has to act. It must ask itself, is a child capable of using a computer intelligently? Would you trust a computer to the kid next door? To your grocer? And would you feel safe knowing that your pharmacist or even your doctor is using one?

Think about it.

The School Connection

People began to speak of "*higher*" math, with a knowing lilt in their voices. The word spread that occasional use of computers was harmless. Soon users began to speak openly of their computer connections. It was only a matter of time before it hit the schools.

It did and now, as the world knows, hundreds of thousands of children of every socio-economic level of society are into computers.

What To Watch For

How can you tell if your child is using them? Here are ten tell-tale signs a concerned parent can watch for:

SIGNS OF COMPUTER USE IN SCHOOL AGE CHILDREN

1. Are Billy's or Mary's grades suddenly going up?

2. Are they asking questions you can't answer?

3. Do you find traces of computer use in their rooms such as half-finished programs, esoteric magazines, and arcane print-outs?

4. Have their appetites changed? Are they suddenly into such things as Chinese food and late-night snacking?

5. Are they uncommonly eager to get to their homework?

6. Is their speech direct, unslurred, and hard to understand?

7. Looking into their eyes — are their pupils bright?

8. Are new friends popping up, kids you'd normally associate with glasses, notebooks and *cleverness*?

9. Are your phone bills getting bigger, with mysterious calls to faraway places late at night even though when you pick up the receiver all you hear is beeps?

10. Do they save their money, work at odd jobs to earn it and then suddenly rush "downtown" to make a "buy."

> **WARNING:**
> *If you suspect your child is using computers and need help to know what to do about it, call your local Computer Hotline where trained social workers will help you ease the burden of knowing that your kid is hooked.*
> **SURGEON GENERAL**

COMPUTERHOLICS ANONYMOUS

A nation's shame — The computerholic ward at General Hospital.

Hope for the Hopelessly Addicted

His name is simply "Joe." Once a highly successful and respected businessman married to a former beauty queen and the father of 2.3 wonderful children, "Joe" fell prey to the evils of computerism while still a young man. His story is an inspiration to everyone who knows someone or has a loved one addicted to computers, "the 20th Century illness" nobody talks about.

The Hell of "Devil ROM"

The path between "Joe's" early, successful career, and his recovery from "Devil ROM" is not a pretty one. It is strewn with the corpses of billions of androids, Kongs, Pacmen, and other electronic horrors. It is littered with unreadable manuals too arcane to understand and too many to count. It is papered with programs that would not run. It is cluttered with the detritus of data crunching that was meaningless and that turned on his coffeemaker when it should have opened his garage door. In brief, "Joe's" solitary sojourn was a journey into Hell. That he recovered is a miracle. But recover he did, even though his story is heart-wrenching.

"Joe" Was Really "Joe Average Guy"

"Joe" was never very good at math. When the first computers were introduced in the '50's, while "Joe" was just a boy, "Joe's" ambition was to be a fireman. Later, in college, he met lovely "Linda." They were married when they were seniors. "Joe" graduated from college. He went to work for Farley Framastan and Widget Corporation as a salesman while "Linda" stayed home and dusted.

"Joe's" winning smile and pleasant manner put him on the fast track to the top at FFWC. Soon he was their crack salesman (in 1963 "Joe" sold more cracks than all the rest of the force combined).

The Beginning of the End

"Joe" had to spend much of his time on the road. At night, lonely and tired and far from home, he would relax in his motel room reading car magazines. Then, in the early '70's a fellow salesman from a company which will not be named suggested "Joe" stop by his room. "Joe," trusting as only a salesman can be, had no idea of the disaster that lay ahead.

The salesman, "Bill," opened his case. In it was a gleaming new pocket calculator. "Like to try sum?" the salesman asked. The rest of the story is too sordid to detail. ▷

Counting on your fingers again is the start of the long road back from computerholism.

"Joe Was Hooked"

"Joe" did try sum. And to his surprise he found that with the amazing little battery operated device, he could. He was hooked. He spent his next paycheck on a calculator of his own. He bought a booklet that explained how to use it. And, to "Linda's" dismay, the first night home, he took the calculator to bed with him.

In no time "Joe" was spending more time with the calculator than with his children. Their plaintive cries of "Where's daddy?" caused "Linda" to turn to women's magazines. It was the beginning of the end for the perfect family, but nobody recognized it.

It's Never Enough

Soon a calculator wasn't enough. "Joe" invested in a small computer. He was into the hard stuff. "It's not so hard," his already addicted friends told him. They were a new crowd "Joe" was hanging around with. He forsook his old friends for men who were more interested in machines than people.

By the time "Bobby" and "Lisa" were teenagers, "Joe"

The Help key is the coward's way out.

---

was spending his time and his quarters at the corner video game store. The two lovely children would call in through the open door, through the drifting smoke and loud shouts of men who'd lost their reason, for their father to come home. But "Joe" was too far gone.

The Secret

"Joe" began to secretly use the computer at the office. On weekends he would hole up in his room with his growing array of peripherals while his family prayed downstairs for deliverance for their lost leader.

Then one ugly Monday morning "Joe" found himself crumpled up on the couch. His head ached. His eyes were sore. His fingertips were raw. He struggled to the bathroom mirror, took one look and swore never to compute again.

Victorious, at Last

"Joe's" story is familiar to millions of former computerholics who have followed his inspiration and have quit their debilitating addictions. Now the head of the soul-saving organization he founded, Computerholics Anonymous, "Joe" lives by his motto, "'One day at a time.' To do two days at a time you need a computer."

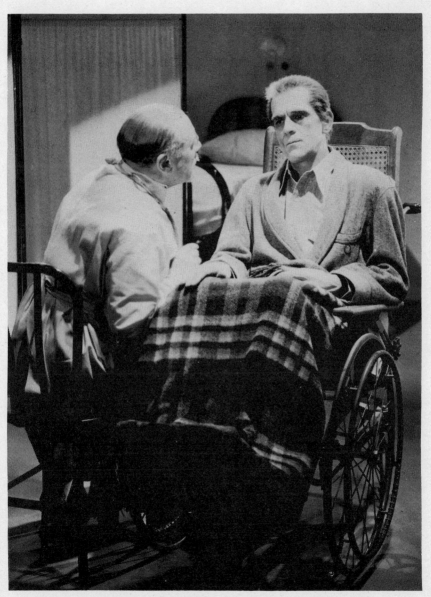

Dr. Herman Mung tells a computerholic the crushing truth —
his brain has gone soft from too much playing with his joystick.

COMPUTER

The Tragedy of

9 - YEAR - OLD COMPUTER COMPANY PRESIDENT LEAPS FROM OFFICE WINDOW

It hasn't happened yet, but how long will it be before the headlines are full of computer tragedies involving elfin executives? Not long at the rate children are being indoctrinated into the cut-throat world of computers.

There was a time when the world was still a safe place to breathe the air and drink the water, that a child was given child's things to pass the long hours between Cap'n Crunch in the morning and cookies and milk in the afternoon. Shedding, one-eyed Teddy bears and Dribbling Debby dolls, red coaster wagons with rubber tires and baby buggies with rubber bumpers were the kinds of things good little boys and girls found in their Christmas stockings or in their birthday cakes.

The beauty of those bygone gifts was that they were so utterly simpleminded that a kid could spend years trying to figure out something fun to do with them. In the meantime, Nature being what it is, the child would grow up, turning first into a zit factory, blooming in time into a mouth that can't be shut, and eventually into a fine, upstanding example of young adult, ready to face the world from which he or she had been protected.

Not so any longer. Instead of Busy-Boxes, infants are playing with mock computers. By the time a kid is four he's been through at least two of dad's old pocket calculators, and by the time he enters nursery school, he's ready for the real thing.

BURN-OUT

Too Much, Too Soon

Unlike dumb toys, computers do something. Not only that, they require the kid playing with them to do something. And worse, if the kid knows what he's doing, the computer can teach the kid a thing or two about the real world. Like how to make a buck.

By the time the average computer-wise child reaches 7, he knows there's a whole world out there waiting for him. And he's ready. Programming is a snap, of course. So is inventory control. Understanding a spread sheet is literally child's play. Earnings predictions, new product development, cost cutting, personnel management, investing, and the full range of business skills are within the grasp of he and his computer.

What does a kid with all this power do? The natural thing, of course. He starts his own company. Whether it's a software firm, a consulting service, a video game development group, or just writing programs, by the time the kid's 10, he's making millions.

And then what? Fat cigars? Big cars? Mysterious trips out of town? Meetings with Japanese youngsters? Mergers? Tiny little ulcers? And then, suddenly, but not unexpectedly, a note is passed to him in class from his banker in the back row. He's overextended. He owes millions. The go-kart, the Big Wheel, the customized Flexible Flyer are all taken away. The kid's left alone. He's over the hill. Burned out. Wiped out. And so he jumps.

Not a nice thing.

PULLING THE PLUG

The Heartbreak of AI*
*(Artificial Intelligence)

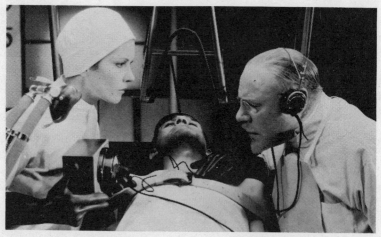

To pull or not to pull. That is the question.

John Hacker (the name has been changed to protect his innocent family from further shame) was a good husband and provider. He held a degree in Accounting, had a good position with a reputable firm, and was in line for a promotion to middle upper middle management, once removed.

John's company was an old-line, traditional firm, a manufacturer of air holes for the brakes in those big trucks that go "whoosh-whoosh." One day the company bought a computer. Because nobody knew how to run it, John was offered the job because he had made the morning coffee for years.

In no time John learned to compute. He began staying late at the office devising bigger and bigger projects for the machine that had come into his life. Soon he was going in on Saturdays. "Just for a few minutes," he would say. It was clear he was becoming addicted, but how was anyone in a small town to know?

John's habit began to rule his life. He began sneaking out of the house on the flimsiest excuses, saying he was going to walk the dog or go downtown to watch somebody get a haircut. What he was really do-ing was secretly visiting a ComputerLand in the "city."

John began to pilfer the milk money his wife left in an empty bottle on the back steps to pay for his habit. He said a rabbit ate it. When the unsuspecting woman shot the rabbit and the money continued to van-ish, John blamed the petty thieving on their young son who they both knew was saving to buy a new crutch.

There was clearly no depth too deep for John to sink to. He even sold his grandmother to a lonely old man.

Eventually John had enough money to buy his own computer. He installed it in a closet in the attic. He began to disappear for long periods of time. Soon he was fired from his job but he didn't tell his wife.

A call from John's office alarmed the poor woman to the tragedy surrounding her. She ran to his tiny cubicle. There, afloat on a sea of plastic hamburger nests from McDonald's and Chinese food con-tainers reeking of MSG, was John, unconscious at his computer, his fingers mindlessly tap-tap-tapping incoherent messages to a hum-ming machine, while thousands of swirling computer bugs covered him like locusts.

The doctor was called and John was rushed to the hospital still plugged into his machine. He had o.d.'d.

John lay in a coma for months. The only thing keeping his bony fingers twitching was the machine. The family was faced with a dread-ful choice; leave the hapless man attached to an Artificial Intelligence Support machine for the rest of his life, or, pull the plug.

The right to make such a decision has been thrown into the courts. But what is a family to do? Who has the power to decide between nor-mal life and AI (artificial intelligence, or, Hacking)? Is it a question for the courts to decide? Who has the right to determine when brain death has occurred in hackers?

There are thousands of similar cases across the land. Each day the newspapers unfold yet another sordid, heart-wrenching story of a devoted son or husband who through ignorance or the desire to "try it just once" gets hooked on computers and o.d.'s on AI.

Nobody knows if there is any normal intelligence left after recovery from AI addiction because, so far, nobody has dared pull a hacker's plug.

When it happens, as it inevitably must, there will be a national uproar. But eventually the dust will settle. The question, Is artificial in-telligence better than no intelligence at all? will be answered.

And when it is, a new, even more difficult question will raise its ugly head, for perhaps the real question is not, Should we pull the plug on some? but, Maybe we ought to plug some others in before it's too late.

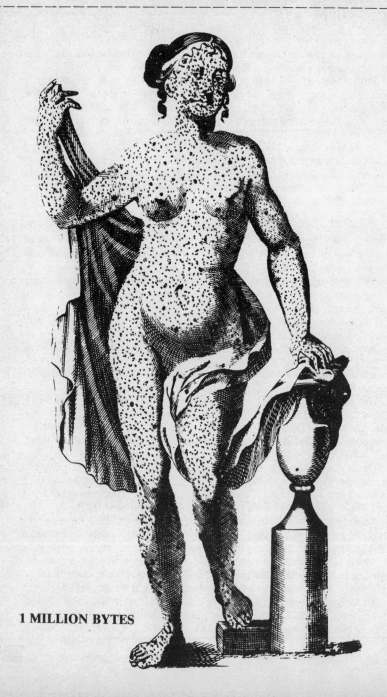

1 MILLION BYTES

HARDWARE, SOFTWARE AND NOWHERE

WHERE WILL IT ALL END

Chapter Seven

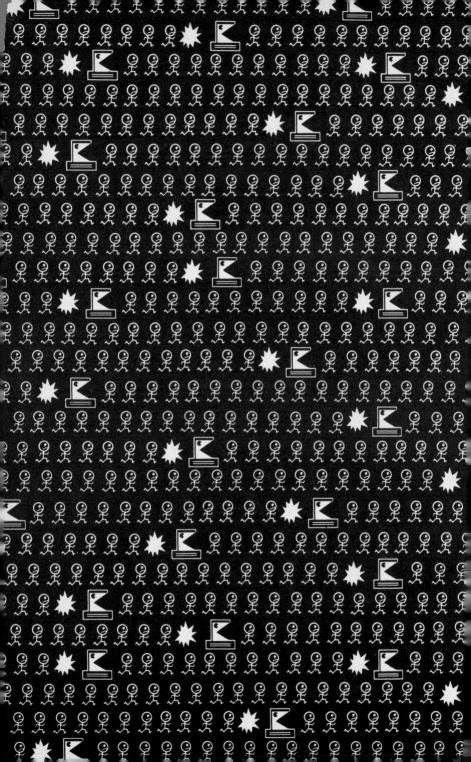

SPACE SHUTTLE

The Ultimate Video Game for Computer Haters

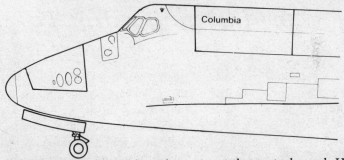

Columbia

Space Shuttle is played in a giant video game machine which is a mock-up of the real space shuttle. Rows of seats fill the shuttle's "pay-load bay." The shuttle's "Mission control center" is in a separate room.

The computer hater player invites computerists, hackers, micro-kids, programmers, computer salesmen and anyone else associated with computers to strap themselves into seats in the shuttle module.

When everyone is in place, the player goes to "Mission control center" and takes his or her place at the control panel. He plays his quarter, which begins the "count-down." When the count reaches "...zero...*blastoff*!" the player punches the FIRE button.

Through the wizardry of the very technology they've created themselves, the passengers on the video space shuttle are blasted into space on wings of fire where they are placed into permanent orbit, never to return again to earth.

The player is then free to pursue the rest of his own life as it was intended.

MOTHER GOOSE VIDEO GAMES

Real World Training for Tots

Advances in video game controls now make it possible for infants to learn the real games of life while still in the crib.

Teaching Baby to Kill

Babes in arms are no longer the odd men out in the fast growing field of creature zapping. In the past babies were limited to pitching bottles of formula across the room, vomiting on unsuspecting laps and hitting rival siblings with rubber ducks to develop the aggressive skills necessary to survive in the dog-eat-dog world of real life. Now, thanks to the mini-microencephalization which predominates in the creative labs of the video games companies, toddlers can learn to kill right along with their older brothers and sisters.

Joy sticks with bootie tops allow infants to firmly grip the controls of the new games with their tiny little feet. An active baby, kicking a mile a minute in its crib, can zap an array of newly designed invaders and enemies, ugly little things which appeal to a newborn's innate sense of disgust, repulsion, hate and urge to kill.

The Three Little Pigs

In *The Three Little Pigs,* the baby in charge plays the part of the Big Bad Wolf. Huffing and puffing electronic blasts of Big Bad Breath, the wolf sets out to destroy piglets by the zillions, turning the little porkers into countless slabs of electronic bacon.

Little Red Riding Hood

The Big Bad Wolf as a role model is used again in the popular, *Little Red Riding Hood.* The object of this clever version of the old fairy tale is to waylay a steady stream of red-cloaked Riding Hoods in an elaborate woods/maze as they struggle to find Grandma's house.

The kicker in this outstanding game is that even if the Riding Hoods reach Grandmas, they are eaten.

Chicken Little

In *Chicken Little* the object is to keep the sky from falling on an electronic chicken who runs frantically back and forth across the bottom of the screen shouting for help. Of course no help is possible, and the game is rigged so the sky falls every time, just like in life.

Other infant games making their debut are such favorites as *Hansel and Gretel* (the kids always get baked in the oven), *Snow White and the Seven Dwarfs* (she dies), and *The Old Woman Who Lived in a Shoe* (overpopulation destroys them all).

A Parent's Pride

Industry spokesmen are enthusiastic about the new games. "They are learning important skills," says Ferdy Pinhead. "Just imagine a parent's pride when Baby says, 'I killed 'leventy seven pigs, goo gah.' "

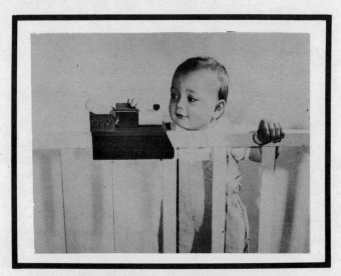

An unsuspecting toddler learns "hands-on" to play Toot, the Little Engine That Doesn't Stop at Crossings for Stalled Buses, *a "hardware" version of the popular video game for children of the same name.*

"There's got to be an easier way to play Dungeons and Dragons than this."

VIDEO GAMES

Kong's Corollary — Never let Life interfere with your game.

Aggression Obsession on a Chip

It's a long way from Pong to Galaxy Annihilator. Pong, that innocuous "*pok-puk*" of yesterday, has spawned a frightening world of vicarious violence. Now anybody can destroy the universe for a quarter.

From simple contests of skill, the video game programmer has developed sophisticated scenarios of death and destruction, in preparation, no doubt, for Arming for Armageddon, the video game the big boys play.

The leap to galactic destruction has left a huge gap in the potential of video games. Space invaders and aliens still have about them a fiction that makes destroying them less than satisfying.

To fill the killer chip gap, a new variety of more realistic and down-to-earth games of derangment is needed before the pacifists learn how to program.

Bad Dad — When Dad refuses to let Junior have the keys to the family car, Junior locks Dad in a dungeon in the cellar. To get out, Dad has to swim through a moat filled with sharks, climb a stairway filled with tumbling boulders, and run across a lawn chased by hundreds of ravenous power lawnmowers. To keep the game realistic, the car is gone every time Dad reaches the garage.

Bomb Mom — A simple game even the kiddies can enjoy. Mom runs back and forth across the bottom of the screen while hundreds of little babies fall toward the ground. If she doesn't catch them in her apron before they hit, they burst. As an added bit of fun, a stack of dishes keeps piling up in the corner which Mom must wash and dry.

Ruin June — A wedding game. Young couples on their way to church are hit by torrential rains, run out of gas, get mugged and change their minds about each other, while ex-beaus chase them in souped-up cars screaming, "If I can't have you, nobody will." If they reach the church, it gets torched by militant altar boys.

Farmer Harmer — Old Mac-Donald tries to get things to grow but every time something pops up from the bottom of the screen, a hailstorm smashes it flat. His herd of cows is killed by lightning bolts from above, and every time Old MacDonald goes to the bank for a loan, the rates go up. To keep things hopping, he is eaten by a flock of cannabalistic chickens.

Tramp Gramp — Gramp hobbles through a maze called Social Security looking for his check. Whenever he reaches the check it gets so small he can't see it. In the middle of a play, Gramp scurries around looking for a men's room while chased by a band of muggers. The object of the game is to get Gramp to his check before it floats away, or him to the men's room before he does.

☆ ☆ ☆ ☆ ☆ ☆ ☆ ☆ ☆ ☆ ☆ ☆ ☆
☆ **Questions to Ask When** ☆
☆ **Shopping for a** ☆
☆ **Computer** ☆
☆ 1. Why is it gray? ☆
☆ 2. How many channels does it ☆
☆   get? ☆
☆ 3. Is this all of it? ☆
☆ 4. Are these 45's or Long Play- ☆
☆   ing? ☆
☆ 5. Is it as easy as it looks? ☆
☆ 6. Are you sure it's on? ☆
☆ 7. Why does it write in green? ☆
☆ 8. Why is the typewriter in two ☆
☆   pieces? ☆
☆ 9. How does it know what to ☆
☆   do? ☆
☆ 10. Do I need to buy anything ☆
☆   else? ☆
☆ ☆ ☆ ☆ ☆ ☆ ☆ ☆ ☆ ☆ ☆ ☆ ☆

Teecher Creature — Hundreds of little first graders are locked in a room when Teecher, a 12-foot monster with jaws on both sides of its head, enters. The player must get the children to the window, where they have the option of jumping or doing homework, before Teecher gets them. After 500 kids jump, Big Bully enters and shoots Teecher with a zip gun. Another Teecher enters with Vice Principal and the game is over. ▷

CHIPS

Or Pieces, or . . . ?

The hottest news out of Silicon Valley is that microchips may not be chips at all.

Though computerists commonly refer to the little devils as ''chips,'' a hotly debated question still rages that technically they are not.

The last laugh will be with computer haters if so called ''chips'' really turn out to be

Flecks

Chunks

Chunklets

Shards

Specks

Bits

Crumbs

Motes

Particles

Particlets

Dabs

Grains

Snips

Jots

Whits

Scraps

Snippets

Slivers

Shreds

Dusts

Grits

Granules

or just simply, itty bitty things.

Granny Cranny — The screen is completely blank when you play your quarter. Then Granny wanders aimlessly in from a corner looking for a place to live. Lovely houses appear out of nowhere. They are owned by her children. But when she reaches them the doors slam shut and the house disappears. The object is to find a cranny to stick Granny in before Buryin' Bob finds her and hauls her away in his big black truck.

Wild Child — Hundreds of hyperactive children pour onto the screen from all sides. They hop and jump and jiggle and won't stand still. Doctor Chemical chases them and must catch them one by one to tranquilize them before Mom and Dad come home. But each time Doc Chemical treats a Wild Child, it splits its personality and becomes two. If Doc succeeds in calming all his little electronic patients, Grandma sends them a box of sugar and the fun starts over.

Other games in development include **Fun Nun,** a game where the kids get the rulers, **Homeroom Tomb,** where the teachers are bricked into a little red schoolhouse and can't get out, and **Cruel School,** where the principal is devoured by thousands of ravenous bookworms.

COMPUTER CRIME

The case of the infamous Dalton Gang caper in New York City is just a forerunner of what computerization of the underworld will bring.

A handful of preppy computer freaks at the exclusive Dalton School managed to access the computer of a large legitimate business and thoroughly shake up its management before the caper was uncovered, using the school's own computer to pull off the job.

The implications for honest crooks are frightening. An 8th grade education will no longer qualify a criminal for even the most rudimentary entry-level position in crime. Graduation from prep school will be mandatory. An applicant will be required to have at least some hands-on experience with computers. His resume won't be considered if he can't program in BASIC. The requisite language skills for communicating with a computer will leave those with rudimentary criminal vocabularies out of work. "Stick 'em up," "Put the money in the bag," and "I've got a gun in my pocket" simply don't work when accessing a bank's computer from three thousand miles away.

Unless the computerization of the way we live is stopped now, a life of crime will be denied to the misfit kid on the block who learned his trade shaking down first graders for their lunch money. Instead, crime will be the province of the educated, to be perpetrated by men in white collars from within the oak-panelled offices of respectable business.

As hard as it is to imagine such a thing as "white collar crime," to coin a phrase, it is possible if computers fell into the wrong hands.

Keep crime in the hands of the criminals.

The Truth About E.T.

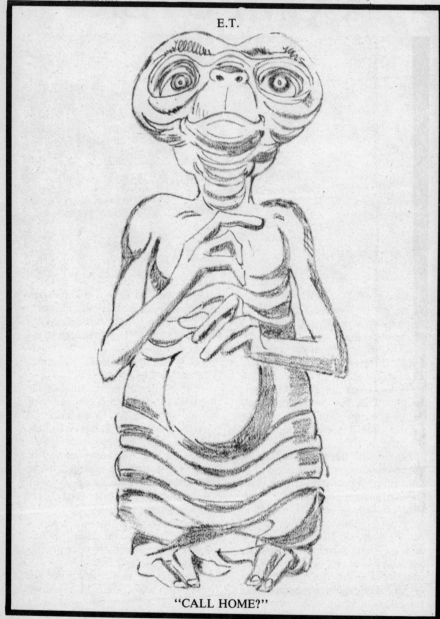

E.T.

"CALL HOME?"

E.T. was not a computerized robot

X RAY.

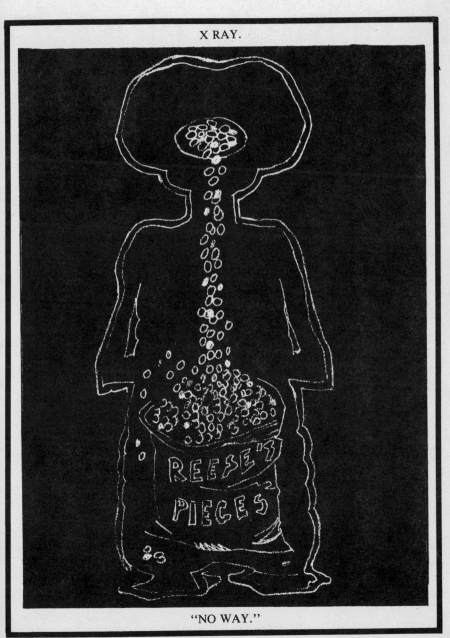

"NO WAY."

as shown in this X-ray view.

HOW TO BREAK THE VIDEO GAME HABIT

GET THE VIDEO GAME...

Arcade addicts need help. They are slaves to their passion, foils of their fantasies, and a burden to their parents, friends, family and society.

The quarters that addicts daily feed into arcade video game machines are desperately needed to keep the wheels of mechanized America turning. Each quarter plugged into a video game is one less quarter for a toll booth, a cigarette machine, an automatic washer in the dorm basement, a gumball machine at a shopping plaza, a soft drink dispenser at a movie theatre, a peep show viewer, a tabletop jukebox, a comb dispenser in a Howard Johnson's men's room, a play on an Eerie Digger at the county fair, or a down payment on Eternity in the Sunday collection plate.

The diversion of quarters from essentials to frivolous pursuits has to stop. The only way to redirect the flow is to stop the addicts from wasting them on arcade video games.

Help addicts help themselves. Save a quarter today. Here's how.

1. Cut holes in the bottom of the addict's pocket. The quarters may roll out on the ground, but at least they'll still be in circulation.

2. Heat all quarters lying around the house until red hot. It makes them tough to put in the Laundromat, but at least *you'll* know to wear gloves.

3. Paint the edges silver. Addicts are easily fooled. If they can believe a little electronic gizmo is really a space ship, they'll believe all the silver-edged quarters are real silver and save them.

4. Mix rubber quarters in with the normal ones. The frustration of trying to stick a floppy quarter into a slot will kill the urge to play.

5. Tie long thin threads to all his quarters. Hold the other end. When you feel the quarter slipping into a slot, jerk it back.

6. Glue two quarters together. They won't fit into any slot and you can always pry them apart when you need butts.

7. Cast a handful of lead quarters. Your addict will eventually get caught playing these slugs. He'll be arrested and thrown into jail. This is extreme, but it'll keep him out of arcades.

8. Melt ripe cheese over his quarters. Nobody will go near him when he plays. Since half the fun of addiction is having an audience watch you build a score, the desire to play will go away.

9. Freeze individual quarters into ice cubes. By the time he thaws the thing his hand will be numb, he won't be able to play anyway.

10. Cut off his fingers.

...BEFORE IT GETS YOU.

KOMPUTER KAMPS FOR KOOKS

High Tech Rec, or, Fun Without the Sun

Computer nerds aren't born, they're made. The logical time to make them is when they are young and still too wet behind the chips to know any better.

What's a Parent To Do?

What's an over-achieving parent to do with a kid who's already past six years old and still shows no interest in the Computer Revolution? Write them off and send them to dental school? Hope they get work bagging groceries at the local market? Set them up as drug dealers? Hope they can learn enough to teach?

A really concerned parent quickly realizes there are very few career choices left that don't require a background in computers.

There Is an Answer

Fortunately there is an answer to the question, "What can I do to remind this freckle-faced kid that Life isn't a free ride of baseball cards, Froot Loops, fishin' for bullheads and waiting to find out why girls are different?" It's the *computer camp*.

Computer Camps Are *Fun*

Computer camps are *fun*. Combining the worst of two traditions, summer camps and computers, they are frequently situated in abandoned mining camps, remote forest ranger bivouac areas, and other uninhabited, unreachable outposts where bugs practice cannibalism and the air is permanently cooled to match the temperature of the lake, an invigorating 33 °F.

Summer camps are located on mountain peaks and at the ends of bottomless canyons for a reason. Parents who shipped their tots off to the boonies could be reasonably certain of a quiet summer for as long as it took the kid to find his way back to civilization. The fact that mail and phone service to the edge of the earth was nonexistent to laughable was also a factor parents considered for their peace of mind.

The Making of a Hermit

As it turned out, the natural isolation of summer camps was also perfect for nurturing the total estrangement from fellow humans that computer nerds thrive on. Tucked away for weeks and months at a time with only the company of a beeping machine and the occasional visit of a curious hermit, computer clones quickly learn the odd habits they will need to survive for months alone in their rooms, offices and eventually labs without once having to see the real world.

Computer Hi-Jinks

Computer camps are not without heart, however. The great traditions of summer camp practical jokes have been reprogrammed to fit the hilarious sense of humor consistent with kids who find it outrageously comical to calculate the predicted crash zones of failing Russian satellites and then call the unsuspecting inhabitants of the region and shout over the phone, "You're gonna die!" Indeed, what chiphead ▷

The quality of life at Computer Camp compares favorably with living atop a toxic waste disposal site.

could forget the great fun of putting a dead program in his bunkmate's sleeping bag? Or short-sheeting the tractor feed on the camp director's printer? Or tying the camp's star jerk's fingers together while he's sleeping so he couldn't punch an entry when he wakes up? Or the all-time classic gag of putting program disks in the wrong sleeves. What a rip!

A Narrow Mind in a Weak Body

Computer camp isn't all fun and games. Although the emphasis is on a narrow mind, a

Kampers learn anal retentive traits to prepare for the rigidly disciplined life of a programmer.

devastated body is just as important for hackers who will spend the rest of their lives without seeing the sun, eating a decent meal, or moving out of their chairs. Computer camps encourage a full complement of hacking-related sports.

Some of the favorite recreational pastimes are Staring at Squiggly Lights for Long Periods, Sitting Until Numb, Head Scratching, Chin Stroking, and, of course, Manifold Paper Origami.

Nutrition is a challenge for computer camp cooks, but the challenge is always met. Parents who visit on Parents' Day are often delighted to learn that their Junior or Sissy has learned to live on Coke, Twinkies, dried sandwiches and fortune cookies. They know their tiny nerds will have no culinary disappointments adjusting when they grow up to be hackers.

Computer camp isn't for everybody, just as computers aren't for everybody. Thank goodness.

Parents write:

"I sent Herky to computer camp because he was starting to talk to people."

"We sent him because we heard they didn't come back."

"He was turning onto books. What else could we do?"

KOMPUTER KAMP KORNER

The Berkshire Bytes For Tykes Computer Camp-

Total isolation. Johnny won't find his way home, ever. Staff of 20 anti-social hackers on duty 24 hours. Free arcade. 8 million versions of Donkey Kong. Video game burnout in two weeks or your tuition back.

Kamp Pentagon-

Actually located in an unused corridor of the Pentagon. Learn real-life situations from live generals, e.g., MegaCalc, the megatonnage calculating game; World Blitz, the hands-on rocket launch program; Buck-Burner, the Defense Department budget—planning game; and, DreamWorld, the ultimate fantasy game. Much ahead of anything the Russians have. Cost: $6 trillion, but worth every penny.

Wally Wall Street's-

The ultimate computer camp. Learn Futurism; predict world collapse; join the Tri-Lateral Commission. All at the end of a two-week intensive. Situated in the heart of Wall Street at 1600 Pennsylvania Avenue, Washington, D.C., Wally Wall Street's Computer Camp is not for the light of heart, compassionate, or terribly intelligent.

Old MacDonald's Farm Camp-

Program hog belly futures. Calculate government subsidies. Simulate real life farming by learning what not to plant and planting anyway. Relax with "Korny Porny," the on-the-farm video game with Little Bo Peep and her weird lamb. Near Peoria.

The Kero-Sum —   The world's first kerosene-powered computer. Built in Pakistan. Used to guide their first-generation missile delivery system.

THIRD WORLD TECHNOLOGY

Keeping Up with the Joneses

Every new idea breeds imitators. Anyone who has put in a backyard pool, bought a snow blower, gotten a divorce or learned to sign knows that within two weeks, everybody on the block is doing the same thing.

The same holds for nations. No sooner had the Vikings discovered America than the Italians started making plans to do the same. The minute the English decided to move to America, everybody followed suit. Within a few years after America developed the nuclear bomb, Russia, France and England followed. Like dominoes, the rest of the world tumbled after so that now even Third World nations, which can scarcely keep their leaders living like kings, are building bombs.

The same will surely be true of computers. Today the computer is made in advanced, technological nations to deal with the sophisticated problems that develop at the cutting edge of the future. But how long will it be before other nations, envious and determined to keep up, will produce computers of their own, for their own future needs? Not long, we suspect.

Beware of Computer Emissions

When a computer is used to calculate, its infamous microchips run through hundreds of thousands of computations a second and then spit out only a single, puny, green answer on its CRT.

What happened to all those other numbers? Where are they?

The answer is, they're still in the machine.

When you do calculations the old-fashioned way with paper and pencil, you *know* where all the extra digits are. They're spread all over the paper like tracks in the snow. And they stay on the paper when you don't need them any longer. They go when the paper goes.

Not so with computers. All the numbers between the question and the answer stay inside the machine. You can't get rid of them because there's a sign on the back that tells you not to open the machine or you'll die.

What happens when the machine can't hold any more used numbers? Boom! *Computer emission.*

If computers aren't stopped now, someday not very far off they'll all dump their numbers at the same time and the world will be buried in used integers.

And people think computers aren't dangerous.

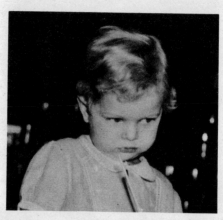

MICROTEENS AND COMPUTERNIKS

Computer Literacy Among Children...America's Disgrace A Case History-

Jennifer Goodheart, age 9, a Brownie, Campfire Girl, Bluebird of Happiness and an Angel in her church choir in Midville, Iowa, returned home from school to find her parents blubbering on the floor. It was not a pretty sight. In Jennifer's father's hand was the monthly bank statement. Her mother clutched a handful of check stubs and cash register receipts in her pitiful grip. Both parents had o.d.'d on red ink.

The Goodhearts were rushed to an accountant. In a few nerve-wracking moments, the accountant put the Goodhearts' books in order. Sadly, when the accountant's bill arrived a few days later, both adults suffered relapses.

The Goodhearts are now in a home for the Fiscally Handicapped. It is not known if they will ever recover the use of their checkbook.

Little Jennifer saw it all. She dropped out of Brownies. She put out her little campfire. She forgot the words to "Rock of Ages." She aged and turned 10.

It wasn't the shock of finding her parents in the advanced stages of fiscal shock that changed Jennifer Goodheart. It was because she knew she could have prevented the tragedy. Jennifer knew how to program.

Jennifer learned programming in the 3rd grade. She was the president of her own software firm, a company she and her little friends started called Software for Chubby Fingers.

Spreadsheets, budgets, billing, invoicing and record - keeping were child's play for Jennifer.

But she never told her mother and father she could do their books because she knew they would be embarrassed.

Jennifer knew that parents don't understand computers.

If Jennifer had not been introduced to computers at such a young age, the tragedy of that awful day might have been prevented. She would have been just as ignorant as her parents. Instead, she is doomed to know more than they, forever.

Jennifer's future is not pretty. She will remain estranged from her parents because neither of them show the slightest ability to understand computers.

Jennifer Goodheart, age 10, is a *computer orphan.*

Jennifer's story is not unique. *Time, Newsweek,* and *Jack and Jill* are filled with similar heart-

breaking tales of children separated from their parents by the computer gap.

Children from computer-broken homes frequently never recover. Instead, they go on to form their own companies, often by the time they are teenagers. By the time they're ready for college they are earning millions; sometimes they become the sole support of their parents, whose plunge into computer oblivion can no longer be checked, even by remedial courses at local community colleges.

The double tragedy of computer ignorance is understood when one realizes that the children of today's computerniks and micro-kids will understand computers while still in their cradles. That will make grandparents look just plain silly when they give their grandchildren a cookie and a tin can to play with on the kitchen floor.

Certainly Nanno and Nanna deserve more than that.

COMPUTER DATING

What You Don't See Is What You Get

Computerized dating services would have you believe that the world is moving too fast to indulge in the old, tried and tested practices of the dating game. Boy meets girl won't work anymore, they believe. Boy first has to meet computer and *then* he can meet girl, who also has been "screened" by machine.

Is it as simple as that? If Love is what makes the world go round, what's going to happen to everything that isn't nailed down when computer dating gets out of hand? Because just as sure as Jobs made little beige Apples, the world's going to stop turning and we're all going to fly off if computer dating takes over.

Computer haters already know that computer dating just doesn't work. Have you ever tried to buy one a Coke? Ask a computer what its sign is and it'll tell you, along with the tide charts and the next time Comet Kahoutek returns.

The consequences of computer dating are numerous and horrendous to consider. For starters, thousands of matchmakers would be out of work, unless they took a crash course in BASIC. Ugly girls wouldn't have to become nuns or volunteer to do good works in leper colonies if

they knew someone was going to be assigned to them by a computer. Guys who couldn't get a date if they worked in a harem would get all the good spots in the back row at the drive-in movie. Singles bars would go broke. And even getting divorced wouldn't pay because a computer would just hook you back up with someone new anyway. Bachelorhood for men or women would be a thing of the past.

But does computer dating work? Is it possible to feed a machine a set of numbers which purports to describe who you are, what you like, what your interests are, and the kind of life mate you seek — and get what you want?

The old fashioned way may be tedious and fraught with danger, heartbreak and unreasonable cost for flowers, chocolates, movies and trips to visit each other's families, but it got the job done for hundreds of years. There's no reason to believe that a computer can do it any better.

There's no such thing as, "I'm going to mess around with my computer for a few minutes before dinner, dear."

THE COMPUTER COOKBOOK

What You Got Is What You Get

A software program for young cooks on the run, *The Computer Cook* has the operator enter everything left over in the refrigerator and on the kitchen shelves into the computer's memory. The computer then concocts imaginative recipes of whatever ingredients are available.

Touted as a boon to busy people with little time and cast iron stomachs, computerized recipe making may create more of an adventure in dining than the clever cook had in mind.

Based on the contents of the average household refrigerator/kitchen shelf collection of cans, bottles, boxes and bags of wonderful things from the store, some of which have been there since Woodstock, *The Computer Cook* was tested and came up with the following items to add interest to a meal and animated conversation for the guests once they leave.

TURKEY CARCASS CUTLETS

A perfect dish to get rid of the bony hulk that takes up two shelves of the fridge. Turkey Carcass Cutlets are easy to prepare, a surprise to serve, and a curiosity to eat.

To prepare, pulverize turkey carcass with dried stuffing and flaps of old skin still intact in a butter churn. When only a fine gray powder and a few ragged bones are visible, add the crust off gravy tureen forgotten in the back of refrigerator, two boxes of Chinese noodles, a half dozen broken taco shells and a can of pumpkin pie filling. Mix into a thick paste. Let dry for 20 minutes in microwave oven. Slice into thin strips. Fry in old salad dressing. Serve on stale doughnuts.

GRANOLA GAZPACHO AMANDINE

A flavorful mix of what's left in seven opened boxes of cereal, a handful of Christmas nuts and cookies, a can of stewed tomatoes in a base of tonic water, this culinary delight is sure to cause comments for many days after it's eaten.

To prepare, pour cereal and tonic into a blender and blend for 20 minutes. Plop in tomatoes. Boil for 2 minutes. Serve in Styrofoam coffee cups. Garnish with Christmas cookie crumbs.

Serves hundreds.

APPLE ONION PIE

Sure to be a favorite with the grandmothers of tomorrow, Apple Onion Pie can be prepared in minutes. To a freezer-burned prepared pie crust, add filling made from the contents of the vegetable crisper drawer. Include 3 withered apples sliced wafer thin and 4 onions found sprouting in back of potato drawer. Add enough Kool-Aid to moisten.

For an added delight, cover top of pie with mashed potato slices garnished with olives, a dollop of cream cheese with the blue fuzz left on, and sprinkle liberally with radishes.

Other Dishes from
The Computer Cook

Mustard and Lime Prune Whip
Fried Eggs with Mince Meat Sauce
Bacon Fat à la Hamburger Helper
Duncan Hines Chocolate-Baked
  Bean Clusters
7-Up, Macaroni and Cheese Slurry
Sour Cream-Coconut-Artichoke
  Heart Drops

100 THINGS A COMPUTER CAN'T DO

When You Start to Feel Insecure, Remember. A Computer Can't:

1. Keep you warm on a cold winter night.
2. Lick a stamp.
3. Tell you if your tie is straight.
4. Walk the dog.
5. Share your stock losses.
6. Clean the barn.
7. Smile, and mean it.
8. Churn butter.
9. Kiss with any degree of sincerity.
10. Make chicken soup for you when you feel poorly.
11. Find a cop when you need one.
12. Change diapers on a wet baby.
13. Carry your golf clubs.
14. Take your SAT's for you.
15. Fix a flat.
16. Make a really dry martini.
17. Grind meat into hamburger.
18. Turn lead into gold.
19. Lose weight.
20. Lay bricks.
21. Rub its CRT and tap its keyboard at the same time.
22. Bob for apples.
23. Give blood.
24. Give a decent haircut.
25. Throw a slider.
26. Shell peanuts.
27. Spit into the wind.
28. Run your laps for you.
29. Understand cats.
30. Appreciate caviar.
31. Find your reading glasses.
32. Take out the trash.
33. Haul the ashes.
34. Tell the difference between butter and margarine.
35. Use an electric razor or buy the company.
36. Spare you 50¢ for a cup of coffee.
37. Ponder the reason for cockroaches.
38. Tell the difference between a badger and a badge.
39. Pay your taxes after calculating them.
40. Tell you if your fly is open.
41. Play "Melancholy Baby."
42. Tell if someone in the theatre took off their shoes.
43. Bring back vaudeville.
44. Bring back John Wayne.
45. Catch a cold. Cure a cold.
46. Say "Bless you" when you sneeze.
47. Come up with a good reason why you're late for class.
48. Appreciate the irony in Ronald Reagan.
49. Hang wallpaper straight the first time.
50. Tell the difference between *Time* and *Newsweek*.
51. Wonder what Walter Cronkite is doing tonight.
52. Light up a Muriel.

53. Understand why not to drink the water in Mexico.

54. Be curious about Dolly Parton.

55. Get supply side economics to work.

56. Write an ode to a Grecian urn.

57. Respond to the aroma of baking bread.

58. Send a meaningful Valentine.

59. Introduce you to the blond at the end of the bar.

60. Stamp out a forest fire.

61. Cure cancer.

62. Yodel.

63. Write an intelligent letter.

64. Get a bill right the first time.

65. Make small talk at the water cooler.

66. Lay an egg.

67. Do an imitation of Henry Kissinger.

68. Blow smoke rings.

69. Bail out Chrysler Corporation.

70. Talk its way out of a parking ticket.

71. Give mouth to mouth resuscitation.

72. Slice bread.

73. Get into Harvard.

74. Knit a tea cozy.

75. Get rid of ring around the collar.

76. Worry.

77. Laugh at the mention of "chicken" or "prune. "

78. Care who shot J.R.

79. Send flowers.

80. See through Frank Sinatra.

81. Be embarrassed by Preparation H commercials.

82. Leave election forecasting alone.

83. Fill a mail order purchase accurately.

84. Juggle.

85. Jiggle.

86. Pontificate.

87. Understand the Japanese.

88. Design an Edsel.

89. Eat an anchovy.

90. Visit Peoria.

91. Make jokes about the U.S. Postal Service.

92. Justify the re-commissioning for the third time of the *New Jersey*.

93. Balance the budget.

94. Enjoy the sunset.

95. Produce the names of more than three people who speak Esperanto.

96. Remember when Orson Welles was played by just one man.

97. Understand the logic of the N.R.A.

98. Think of something interesting about North Dakota.

99. Get excited about Comet Kahoutek.

100. Think.

Computer Firm Names Board of Directors

BANANA Computer Corporation president Tommy Tasks recently announced the appointment of his third grade class as board of directors of his multi-million dollar company which he founded in a treehouse with his playmate, Goober.

The directors, all computer experts, had this to say about the future of computers, "Wow, gosh, gee, golly, shucks, gee whiz!"

LET'S GET ORGANIZED

Computer Haters International, or, CHI, appropriately symbolized by the Greek letter X, was founded in 1957 by Kent Reade-O'Wright, an undergraduate at MMU (Mickey Mouse University, the educational arm of Disneyland — with campuses at Disney World and EPCOT Center).

Wright, a student of Numbers Theory (the theory: *There are no such things as numbers and, even if there were, nobody would understand them or care anyway*) was among the very first of the nation's college students to have his class schedule worked out by a computer, an instrument very much in its infancy in the aboriginal Fifties when dates were still made in person over Coke that you *drank* through a straw and automatic washers had two cycles, *off* and *on*, which were controlled by people, not chips.

Class Scheduling the Old-Fashioned Way

Prior to the advent of the computer at MMU, students' class scheduling was done the old-fashioned way, by lengthy discussion ▷

over wine and crackers in front of a crackling fire in the library of one's faculty advisor.

A typical scheduling session went as follows:

Faculty Advisor (Often the Dean of Students if the President was busy tutoring Freshman English): Well, Kent, what do you think you'd like to do with the rest of your life? And by the way, please try another glass of this *Medoc,* 1947. It's excellent. Cheese?"

Kent (His head resting on Faculty Advisor's daughter's lap, who is dropping fresh grapes into *his mouth):* Thank you, Professor, I don't mind if I do. By the way, the *Chateauneuf du pape* was superb. Well, I've given my future a great deal of thought and I've decided that I'd like to be healthy, wealthy and wise, and maybe meet some great chicks."

Faculty Advisor: You're quite a philosopher, Kent. An excellent plan. I've worked out a preliminary schedule of courses for you that fits your requirements for a comfortable life, perfectly. I'm recommending 3 credits for your first semester; my own course, *Grappling with Innuendo.* Next

CAVEAT EMPTOR
To the untrained eye, this APPLE looks perfect.

But lurking inside, visible only to a trained expert, is a "bug."

semester I suggest you take *Watching for Halley's Comet* to satisfy your Science requirements, and, *The Sports Page as Literature,* to complete your English obligation. Cigar?"

The Road to Success Opens

Following three or four similar counseling sessions, an undergrad's schedule would contain nothing to conflict with his future plans. He could comfortably graduate (Minima Cum Lader) with a Degree in Generalities and be ready to face a benign world where a handshake, a smile, and a few kind words were all he would need to embark on the road to success.

Kent Reade-O'Wright was certain he could carry the load recommended by his advisor in that watershed year, 1957. Little did he know.

And Closes

MMU acquired one of the very first Meaniac IV Digital Computers that very fall of Kent's entry into Life. With it, Kent's and everybody else's world changed. The machine's first task — after it was used to mismatch every single pair of socks in the student laundry — was to create perfect course schedules for everyone enrolled at MMU.

Computerized Class Schedules Via IBM

When Kent received his IBM punch cards in the mail, he found he was signed up for *Open Heart Surgery* 312 (as a volunteer patient), *Binomial Interdigital Unicomplexitory Integral Calculus* 100, *Conversational Hittite* 411, and *Women's Stick Ball.* He rebelled.

"Computers aren't going to run my life," Kent said. "I run my life."

The sentiment caught on quickly among Kent's bewildered classmates, some of whom had never yet dated a key-punch operator but who already knew how cold and calculating they could be in their impersonal detachment from reality.

The First Anti-Computer Rally

"Something has to be done to stop computers or they'll take over the world," Kent exclaimed at an anti-computer rally — the first of its kind, but not the last as the burgeoning legions of cynical anti-cyberneticists quickly learned, cf. *The March on White Plains (street riots and name calling at IBM headquarters) 1963; Students Revolt for Names, not Numbers, 1971; Ad Hoc Ban the Chip Symposium, Geneva, 1982;* ▷

The Trial of the Silicon Valley 7 (citrus farmers squeezed out by circuitry), 1983; et al.

Computer Haters Organized at Last

A nucleus of hard-core computer haters was formed with Kent Reade-O'Wright as its leader. A slogan was adopted, *"Computers Don't Rule the World...People Rule the World."* A symbol, CHI (X), was chosen, and the first membership cards were issued. Lapel pins, a black X on a stark white background, began to appear on campuses everywhere. A Loyalty Oath (*"I do not now nor have I ever understood computers"*) was inspired by the Senate Un-Numerical Investigations Committee Hearings (*Chairman, Sen. Joe McGoogol — "Mr.*

Chairman, Mr. Chairman, Decimal Point of Order!").

Ban the Computer

"Ban the Computer" soon became a rallying cry in the real world of commerce, business, industry and housework as well as in the ivied ivory towers of education. By 1976 over a great many people were members of CHI; the number is expected to get larger by at least more by the year 2000.

What started as one man's quiet rebellion against outside forces destroying his life, something which he fervently believed was everyone's God-given right to accomplish on one's own, without machine intervention, grew into a *Movement*.

Kent Reade-O'Wright now lives in South Dakota, where he oversees the daily operation of CHI and writes inspirational tracts in longhand on the dangers of International Computerism.

"I'm worried about Junior. He's been up in his room since Christmas of '81 with that computer you gave him."

How to Join

To join Computer Haters International (CHI), complete the following application in longhand and send it to:

Computer Haters International
Last Chance Ranch
Hope Springs
Eternal, S.D. (letters with zip codes will be returned to sender)

COMPUTER HATERS INTERNATIONAL
Membership Application

The undersigned hereby requests admission as a member in good standing to CHI.

Name _____
        First   Last   Always

Address _____
        Real World Only, i.e., NO ZIP CODE

(CHI considers all other information, whether personal or not, to be your business. Membership lists are not sold to anybody for any reason; do not expect unsolicited magazine salesmen to call.)

_____

Computer Haters International Pledge (CHIP)

"I, _____, the sole control of a sound mind and body, and possessing enough fingers and toes to do all the digital computing I need to know to keep approximate track of my age, to understand a 'Home vs Visitors' scoreboard, to calculate a luncheon bill to the nearest 'close enough,' to figure out for myself if it's dark out and it's time for me to turn on the lights, and to determine by brainpower alone when and if I want to plunge the world into war, do hereby pledge to do everything within my power to keep computers out of my life by fair means or foul and to work for their self-destruction by pretending to go along with them until it's time for us to strike back."

NEW COMPUTER DESIGNS
Computer Designs We'd Like to See

The better made a computer is, the longer it will last. The longer computers last, the longer they will continue to rule the lives of computer haters.

As a compromise, the following computer designs are recommended to help maintain the balance between people and machines. After all, if people eventually wear out, why shouldn't a computer?

The Ice Computer — Made of pure ice that immediately melts when it is plugged in to leave nothing but a damp spot on your desk and a satisfied smile on the would-be user's face.

Rubik's Computer —　Designed by Rubik, this ingenious device comes unassembled and can be put together in over ten trillion ways, but nobody can do it before becoming completely frustrated, and so they quit trying.

The Doughnut Computer — Made of freshly fried doughnut dough, bits and pieces can be torn from it and dunked into one's morning coffee. Lasts only three days before going stale and can no longer be softened, even by soaking.

The Silly Putty Computer — Formed entirely from gobs of Silly Putty, this computer drools off your desktop before you can plug it in.

The Jelly Bean Computer — Placed conspicuously on a desk, its components are eaten by passing office workers and Presidents before anyone can sit down at it long enough to use.

The Knit Computer — Made of virgin wool by well-intentioned grandmothers, each computer has a loose end which snags easily to unravel the whole thing.

The Television Set Computer — Disguised to look exactly like a Sony, it is stolen within minutes of placing it on your desk.

The Cat Computer — Made of real cats, it looks pretty sitting on a desktop, but the minute you sit down to use it it stretches, hisses at you and walks away.

COMPUTERSPEAK
Chapter Eight

COMPUTERSPEAK

It's as easy to understand computers as it is to understand the computerists speaking language of computers. (I.e., you can't understand computers.)

Computerists speak in a highly technical babble that only other computerists comprehend. It gives them a sense of power.

Don't be dismayed the next time you find yourself trapped in a computer conversation by some long-winded hacker who really believes he's at the center of the "Technological Revolution". With a little practice, you can out-finesse him at his own game.

All you need to know are the buzz-words of the business. Since they don't mean anything anyway, use them whichever way suits you best.

On the following pages are some of the most common computer conversation cop-outs, the terms computerists sprinkle into their language to make you think they're saying something really important. Don't believe them for a minute.

Memorize a few bits of ComputerSpeak and you'll be on a conversational par with any of the most erudite salesmen, hackers or run-of-the-mill computerists you'll ever have the ill-fortune to meet.

GLOSSARY

A

Abort — When the bus is full, the conductor shouts, "All abort!"

Absolute Address — Where she really lives, not where she told you she lives.

Absolute Error — To buy a computer.

Access — A large, painful boil on the chips from too much hacking.

A/C Converter — A physician specializing in bi-directional surgery.

Accuracy — Something impossible for programmers to attain.

Adder — The part of a cow that counts how much milk is left.

Address — What binary hackers wear when not wearing a suit.

ALGOL — What you sneak into the punch at hacker parties to liven them up.

Algorithm — An unsteady gait as the result of too much ALGOL.

Alpha — Last name of Little Rascal star, Alf.

Analog — Banana and ice cream treat; good with jimmies.

Alphabetic — A blood condition resulting from too many acronyms.

Ambiguity Error — When something is definitely wrong, or maybe not.

ANSI — A hacker who can't sit still.

Apple DOS — Apple R_x

Arithmetical Shift — Going from 1st to 4th gear *without* skipping 2nd and 3rd.

ARPAnet — The government computer network, i.e., the fine mesh we're in.

Array — Spontaneous exclamation by a hacker when something works for a change; rarely used.

Artificial Intelligence — Anybody who needs a machine to tell them what everybody else already knows, e.g. a computerist.

ASCII — The key to your girl friend's apartment.

Attenuate — Response to cannibal who's eaten the very best and asks you to rate it for him.

Automatic Check — The one you write every month to your software supplier.

Auto-answer — Similar to Dial-A-Prayer, but instead of a clergyman, you get Mr. Good-wrench.

Auto-repeat — A key which, when held down, when held down, when held down . . .

Auxiliary Memory — What you go to when she doesn't believe you were working late at the office, e.g., "The train was hijacked to Cuba."

B

Backward recovery — Reaganomics.

Badge Reader — Convention goer who gets off on reading, "Hi, I'm ..." badges.

Bagbiting — What happens when you don't unwrap your sandwich.

Banks — Quiet, air-conditioned places where your salary is automatically transferred to peripheral salesmen.

Bar Code Scanner — A bouncer who checks the crowd for jackets and ties.

Barrel Printer — The guy who writes XXX on whiskey kegs.

BASIC — Something so "simple" you need a computer to understand it.

Batch — A minor gripe.

Batch Processing — Cleaning up a batch so you can say it in mixed company.

Baud Rate — Fee charged by loose women; usually $5.00 and up.

Bell Labs — Large black retrievers that go "Ding-a-ling!" instead of "Bow wow!"

Benchmark — Painful creases pressed into chips from sitting for long periods on park benches.

Bias — Said of Siamese twins, as in, "They've got a cute little..."

Bi-directional — A computerist who swings both ways.

Binary — A little yellow bird that waves instead of whistles.

Binary File — A whole row of them.

Bi-polar — An Eskimo marketing slogan.

Bit — A one, but it doesn't say one *what*, or nothing, so why bother naming it?

Block Moves — What happens when a hacker rents a house on the street.

Block Copy — There goes the neighborhood.

bpi — A gambling term, as in, "You bet your bpi."

Buffer — A nude hacker.

Buffer Amplifier — One who brags about it.

Buffer Store — Where a buffer can't buy a thing to wear.

Bug — A small German car found in American Automakers' computer programs in the '60's.

Burst Speed — The velocity at which hackers' egos pop when confronted by a 12-year-old micro-kid.

Byte — Short for "buy it." Refers to how many peripherals you'll have to purchase to support a computer, e.g., there are 8 "buy it," 16 "buy it" and 64 "buy it" computers.

C

Calculating Punch — To figure out how many drinks a word processor can handle at the office party before she gives you her ASCII.

Card Reader — A gypsy palmist and advisor.

Carriage Return — What you do if you decide not to keep the kid.

Chain Printer — Someone who can't give up printing.

Chip — What one sits on; come in pairs.

Cold Boot — What a programmer puts on feet in winter.

Cold Solder Joint — Marijuana so strong you don't have to light it to put lead in your pencil.

Computer on a Chip — A hacker who sits leaning to one side.

Computer Science — The fastest growing voodoo art course in American colleges and universities.

cps — Refers letter reader to postscript.

Crock — A timing device made in Japan.

Cursor — A hacker who batches a lot.

D

Daisy Wheel — A group of uni-directional buffers sitting in a circle.

Data — A nice-a Italian girl.

Data Base — Where she lives.

Data Bus — What she drives at work.

Decrement — The crap you get from computers.

Dedicated Key — One she gave only to you.

Dedicated Word Processor — A secretary who stays after 5.

Difference Engine — The first thing little boy hackers forget about little girl hackers.

DIP — Abbrev. for Hacker.

Dirty Power — Rallying cry of militant pigs.

Disk Drive — A popular address in Cupertino.

Document — To ask your physician for a clarification of what he intended to say.

Double Density — Really dumb.

Down — Said of computers made of feathers: "That computer is down."

Dumb Terminal — A hacker interfaced with a smart terminal.

Dump — The best place for computers.

E

Eight Bit Chip — A one dollar hooker.

Electronic Mail — Post office jargon for anything delivered in less than a week.

Embed — To spend time with a word processor at her place.

End Users — Hackers who sit a lot.

Ergonomics — How Ronny spells it.

Expansion Slots — The extra holes in your belt buckle.

Execution Time — The time it takes to strangle the salesman who talked you into buying a computer.

F

Fatal Bug — To have a Volkswagen drop on you.

Feedback — To replay what you had for lunch.

Floating Decimal — One which bobs up unexpectedly in a sea of confusion.

Floppy Disc — Serious curvature of the spine.

Fortune Cookie Program — An evening spent at the theatre listening to irrelevant one-liners.

Frequency — Disease suffered by video game freaks.

Friendly — Said of anything associated with computers that is incomprehensible or does not work the way it says it will.

G

Gas Plasma — Residual software stain.

Germanium Chip — Das schwanz.

Gigabyte — A painful sting on the giga.

H

Hacker — A misanthropic bore.

Hard Space — Popular spot between a rock and a hard place.

Head Crash — A collision with a Porta-Potty.

Heuristic — To behave like a heur.

Hexadecimal — A 10-letter Shaker curse.

High-Level Language — An idiom spoken by hackers wearing tights.

Hologram — A salutation to an elderly woman.

Horizontal Scrolling — The missionary way.

I

Increment — What computers eat to produce decrement.

Industry Standards — Non-conforming guidelines.

Integrated circuit — An electric bus with randomly seated black chips.

Intelligent — A hypothetical term in computing.

Interlace — To tie two boots together.

Interpreter — The person you take with you to a computer store to understand what the salesman is talking about; usually a 12-year-old kid.

J

Joystick — A truncheon used by sadists.

K

Keypad — An apartment with a lock.

Keyword — "Your place or mine?"

L

Light Pen — A minimum sentence prison.

Line Feed — "I've never met anyone as interesting as you before," etc.

M

Machine Independent — The goal of all computer haters.

Machine Language — "Zoom, Putt-putt, Chug-a-Chug-a ," etc.

Memory — The part of a computer where data is placed prior to destruction.

Multipass — To try again after she turns you down the first time.

Menu — An itemized list of ways to make a mistake on a computer.

Microminiaturization — "Get small" in computerist's language.

Mnemonic — Said of someone suffering from mnemonia.

Monitor — The first iron-clad CRT.

Multi-processing — To cook statistics more than once.

Multi-programming — To watch all three networks at once.

Multi-tasking — When one "tsk" won't do, e.g., "tsk-tsk-tsk."

Under the most rigorously controlled conditions of pressure, temperature, humidity and other controllable variables, a computer will do what it damn well wants to do.

N

n — After x, the second most popular number that doesn't mean anything.

Nanosecond — A witness to a duel between grandfathers.

Night Mode — Computing in pajamas.

Network — What fishermen do when not fishing.

Non-Impact Printer — One whose signs go unnoticed.

Nybble — What an unsuspecting customer does to a line dangled by a computer salesman.

O

Overstrike — To tempt fate, e.g., Air Traffic Controllers.

Office Information System — The word processor who knows the most gossip.

Ohm — Where the 'eart is.

Operator — A computer salesman. One who sells tape is a reel operator.

Output Device — A word processor who can't say "No!"

P

Papertape Punch — A mushy drink that sticks to the roof of your mouth.

Parabolic Dish — A word processor with all the curves in the right places.

Peripheral — Anything that costs a lot of money that can be remotely associated with computers.

Phase Encoding — A memory trick to remember people by if you can never remember a name.

Pitch — Adding all the characters in an inch of type will give you the sum of the pitch.

Plasma Display — A bloody nose.

Plotter — The computer salesman who spots you browsing during your lunch hour.

Hackerism —
A disease for which there is no known cure.

Polarity — Solidarinoscz.

Program — A random accumulation of bugs.

Program Counter — A parent who limits how much TV you watch.

Q

Query Language — Flippant remarks by mono-directionals.

QWERTY — To be a little strange.

R

RAM — Where most of the bugs are kept.

R&D — Bookkeeping entry for "Uncontrolled expenses."

Raw Data — A nice-a Italian buffer.

ROM — Where you put all the bugs that won't fit in RAM.

Read/Write Head — Men's room with invitational graffiti wall.

Redundancy — Two computer experts when none will do.

Routine — A program that never works the same way twice.

Run — What you should do when a hacker approaches.

Running Head — One which needs the handle jiggled.

S

Search Language — "Seen any good-looking word processors around here?" etc.

Semi-Conductor — One who only takes tickets part time.

Shelf Life — The strange, fuzzy stuff that grows behind books and under beds.

Silicon — A foolish prisoner.

Skew — Interface between consenting computers.

Skew Failure — Premature calculation.

Smart Terminal — The one that gets you to buy it.

Software — What hackers wear under their hardware.

Software House — Frederick's of Hollywood.

Solid State — One that operates without a deficit.

Stack — The part of a word processor where the chips are.

Standard Operating Procedure — The way nobody does it.

Sub-Routine — "Dive! Dive!"

Superfiche — Moby Dick, Jaws, etc.

T

Tape Comparator — A device used to measure who has the longest tape.

Tape Punch — A non-alcoholic drink that comes in rolls and sticks to your fingers.

Teaching Machine — An instructor who doesn't stop lecturing when the class ends.

Telegraph — A plot of teles.

Telepack — A brewery that delivers.

Terminal Intelligence — To be so smart it kills you.

Terminal Transparency — A fatal disease where the sufferer slowly disappears.

Thin Film — A movie with a predictable plot.

Time Sharing — What you do when only one of you has a watch.

Transducer — A seducer in drag.

Transponder — To seriously think about something on the way to the coast.

Those who can, compute. Those who cannot, program. Those who can't program, write manuals; those who can't write manuals sell computers.

U

Ultrafiche — Bigger, faster, and harder to land than superfiche.

Umbrella Information Providers — Weather forecasters.

Unix — Air bearings, i.e., no balls.

V

Variable — Anything with a fixed value.

VDT — Herpes sufferer's coffee klatsch.

Virgin Medium — An oracle who has taken a vow of chastity.

W

Wedged — Said of a computer with software tightly jammed between chips.

Word Processing — To change the meanings of words, e.g., computers are *easy* to understand, when word processed means, computers are *impossible* to understand.

Work Station — A desk with a dumb terminal sitting at a computer.

Y

Y Punch — Fruit juice served in the steam room.

Z

Zero — The sum total of everything good that can be said about computers and computerists.

"If I can program an Apple, I sure as hell can make a clay duck."

How to Fix a Computer